S. HRG. 113–192

CRITICAL MINERALS POLICY ACT

HEARING

BEFORE THE

COMMITTEE ON ENERGY AND NATURAL RESOURCES UNITED STATES SENATE

ONE HUNDRED THIRTEENTH CONGRESS

SECOND SESSION

TO

RECEIVE TESTIMONY ON S. 1600, THE CRITICAL MINERALS POLICY ACT OF 2013

JANUARY 28, 2014

Printed for the use of the
Committee on Energy and Natural Resources

U.S. GOVERNMENT PRINTING OFFICE

86–877 PDF WASHINGTON : 2014

For sale by the Superintendent of Documents, U.S. Government Printing Office
Internet: bookstore.gpo.gov Phone: toll free (866) 512–1800; DC area (202) 512–1800
Fax: (202) 512–2104 Mail: Stop IDCC, Washington, DC 20402–0001

COMMITTEE ON ENERGY AND NATURAL RESOURCES

RON WYDEN, Oregon, *Chairman*

TIM JOHNSON, South Dakota
MARY L. LANDRIEU, Louisiana
MARIA CANTWELL, Washington
BERNARD SANDERS, Vermont
DEBBIE STABENOW, Michigan
MARK UDALL, Colorado
AL FRANKEN, Minnesota
JOE MANCHIN, III, West Virginia
BRIAN SCHATZ, Hawaii
MARTIN HEINRICH, New Mexico
TAMMY BALDWIN, Wisconsin

LISA MURKOWSKI, Alaska
JOHN BARRASSO, Wyoming
JAMES E. RISCH, Idaho
MIKE LEE, Utah
DEAN HELLER, Nevada
JEFF FLAKE, Arizona
TIM SCOTT, South Carolina
LAMAR ALEXANDER, Tennessee
ROB PORTMAN, Ohio
JOHN HOEVEN, North Dakota

JOSHUA SHEINKMAN, *Staff Director*
SAM E. FOWLER, *Chief Counsel*
KAREN K. BILLUPS, *Republican Staff Director*
PATRICK J. MCCORMICK III, *Republican Chief Counsel*

CONTENTS

STATEMENTS

APPENDIXES

Appendix I

Appendix II

CRITICAL MINERALS POLICY ACT

TUESDAY, JANUARY 28, 2014

U.S. SENATE,
COMMITTEE ON ENERGY AND NATURAL RESOURCES,
Washington, DC.

The committee met, pursuant to notice, at 10:09 a.m. in room SD–366, Dirksen Senate Office Building, Hon. Ron Wyden, chairman, presiding.

OPENING STATEMENT OF HON. RON WYDEN, U.S. SENATOR FROM OREGON

The CHAIRMAN. The committee will come to order.

Today the committee will turn its attention to S. 1600, the Critical Minerals Policy Act of 2013.

It has been a pleasure to join Senator Murkowski in negotiating a truly bipartisan bill as evidenced by the 9 Democratic and 8 Republican cosponsors.

We've been joined by 17 of our Senate colleagues, including committee members—Senators Udall, Franken, Risch, Hoeven, Landrieu, and Manchin.

It seems to me, Senator Murkowski, this is a testament to the bipartisan effort to reach agreement and I want to tell you again how much I've enjoyed being part of this bipartisan effort through the negotiations that were held.

As the committee learned in passing the Helium Stewardship Act, our country depends on materials that are not burned or consumed for energy, but are key to many energy technologies, from wind turbines, to batteries, to oil refineries, as well as a host of other technologies. Our country is increasingly dependent on these minerals, to increase efficiency, lower costs, and improve performance of manufactured products in these industries. Without them, many of our essential U.S. industries would struggle to survive.

Critical minerals are minerals which are essential to American industries and may be at risk for supply disruption such as by a small global market or geopolitical complexities.

This legislation tackles these issues head on and most importantly it ensures a steady supply of the materials that are crucial to thousands of good paying American jobs. One of the keys to help putting Americans back to work and to help our businesses in a tough global economy is to get it right with respect to our essential, domestic policies.

If I was going to sum it up in a sentence, I would say our premier challenge is to grow things in America, make things in America, add value to them in America, and then ship them somewhere.

To do that American businesses need access to raw materials in especially, in a high technology area, that means access to what is known as the critical mineral field.

Critical minerals are the key to stronger permanent magnets for wind turbines, for cleaner energy, and electric drive vehicles. They're vital to phosphors which give us more efficient lighting and flat panel displays and also give our military night vision goggles and heads up displays.

Critical minerals are key to rechargeable batteries in hybrid and electric vehicles and the high efficiency motors that power them. They serve as catalysts for fuel cells and for refining automobile fuel. We also know that they're essential for many of our advanced weapon systems, MRI machines, and many other technologies that are vital to America's national and economic security.

Yet for as critical as these minerals are, our country has been dangerously depending on imports from foreign suppliers. The United States imports all, all our rare earth oxides, a special class of critical minerals. In fact, American imports the vast majority of them from a single supplier. Ninety-one percent of our rare earths come solely from China, and our country has seen how dangerous this dependence can be.

In 2009, China choked off the supply of these materials to the rest of the world, restricting exports by 72 percent, causing the prices of rare earths to skyrocket here at home.

Although China currently enjoys near monopoly in the global production of critical materials, we're talking now about both mining and processing, the truth is it didn't used to be this way. I think it's our view, of our bipartisan coalition, that it doesn't have to be this way in the future.

Fifteen years ago the United States was self-reliant for our rare earths. Today China holds only 50 percent of the worlds natural reserves while our country holds about 13 percent according to a recent study by the U.S. Geological Survey.

In fact, a large part of the critical mineral supply shock in 2009 was due to uncertainty about the global distribution of critical minerals. When China began to restrict supply, the rest of the world was in the dark about what the alternative sources of the supply were, and were they even available.

Finally, a crucial but too often neglected part of this supply conversation is minerals processing. Although mining is an important part of the supply equation and S. 1600 encourages Federal agencies to expedite the permitting for new critical minerals extraction, it is the lack of processing capacity transforming the raw materials we pull out of the ground into the high-purity compounds needed for manufacturing. It is that challenge that is my concern and the concern of many experts. In a sense, it is our Achilles heel.

Mining more ore in the United States is not going to reduce our dependence on foreign suppliers if the United States does not develop the processing and refining technologies and infrastructure needed to turn the ore into useful products and then recycle them at the end of their useful lives.

S. 1600 expands the U.S supply of critical minerals by looking comprehensively at the entire domestic supply chain of critical minerals. The bill starts with the identification of which minerals and elements are truly in need of special attention. It then requires the Interior Department to conduct assessments of where those minerals are located and expands research to find more efficient ways of extracting and processing the minerals.

The bill also requires the 2 lead agencies, the Department of the Interior and the Department of Agriculture, to take a fresh look at the permitting process. We ought to make sure, with respect to hard rock minerals, that we're looking at every possible way to reduce delays for mining projects that would extract critical minerals.

The legislation also includes important training programs for our future scientists and the bill includes research programs to extract critical minerals from unconventional sources.

Our witnesses today also represent the entire supply chain from research and education, to mining and processing, to manufacturing the final end products our people use every day. We thank them for testifying.

Two of my colleagues have spent an inordinate amount of time working with the committee trying to deal with both the substance and the politics of putting together a bipartisan bill when sometimes people wonder if the U.S. Senate can order a Coca-Cola, let alone do an important piece of legislation.

I want to commend Senator Murkowski and Senator Udall. We'll recognize Senator Murkowski now, then we want to recognize Senator Udall who also has toiled hard and effectively on this issue.

Senator MURKOWSKI.

[The prepared statement of Senator Dean Heller follows:]

PREPARED STATEMENT OF HON. DEAN HELLER, U.S. SENATOR FROM NEVADA

Chairman Wyden and Ranking Member Murkowski, thank you for holding today's hearing. Mining is integral to Nevada's economy, and we have a proud tradition of leading the nation on mining and mineral research. The legislation we are considering today would go a long way towards bringing federal mineral policy into the 21st Century, and I am proud to be an original co-sponsor of this important legislation.

I would like to also thank Mr. Jim Sims, Vice President of Corporate Communications at Molycorp for being here. The company's Mountain Pass rare earth facility is only about seventy miles south of Las Vegas. The project has been an important economic driver in the region, employing hundreds of Nevadans, during a time where my state continues to lead the nation in unemployment. I have had the pleasure of working with Molycorp while it went through the site expansion permitting process, and I am proud that Nevadans are playing such a leading role in our nation's only rare earth oxide producing facility.

In Nevada and across the country, we have an abundance of critical and strategic minerals that play a vital role in our everyday lives, as well as our nation's economic success and national security. The mining industry is one of the central pillars of Nevada's economy, directly employing thousands of Nevadans. But as many people familiar with mining communities know, the jobs directly at the project sites are just one aspect of their economic impact. The influx of hundreds of mining jobs into local communities ultimately facilitates additional economic growth supporting the mine and the people who work there. Those mine workers need restaurants to eat at, convenience stores to shop at, and places to live. A recent economic study showed that mining provides more than 60,000 direct and indirect jobs in the State producing over $200 million in tax revenue and nearly $10 billion of economic activity annually. That is why, even though Nevada currently has one of the highest unemployment rates in the country, the areas in my state that rely on mining, such as Elko County, have an unemployment rate that is nearly half of the State's average.

I am pleased to join this diverse bipartisan group of senators working to enact the Critical Minerals Policy Act. These reforms can reduce our nation's reliance on other countries for the resources we need to power our economy.

STATEMENT OF HON. LISA MURKOWSKI, U.S. SENATOR FROM ALASKA

Senator MURKOWSKI. Thank you Mr. Chairman.

I do appreciate the fact that you have scheduled up this hearing today and very pleased that we are at this point.

You have noted the bipartisanship that went into constructing this bill and you've mentioned several members of the committee, I appreciate your leadership on it as Chairman, but I particularly want to recognize my friend and colleague Senator Udall who had his own bill in the last session and our folks got together and worked through some of the issues. I think what we have built is a legislative proposal that is good and sound and rational and exactly what should happen in a committee likes this.

So I thank you for the opportunity to hear this this morning and again to Senator Udall my thanks to you for your great cooperation in building what I think is a good bill here.

I think it is somewhat, I suppose serendipitous, maybe it's a little bit presumptuous the bill was numbered S. 1600 and when I think of 1600 I think about the white place down the road here. It is my hope that because our bill really does address such significant issues this critical supply chain it already has 19 members on board in a bipartisan sense I really do think that we can send this down the road this year. That would be a great win for this country, and so I will continue to keep working on this with of my colleagues.

Mr. Chairman you've outlined the contents of the bill very well in your opening remarks. I appreciate particularly your recognition that if we don't have the processing capacity and ability, we are still left in a very, very vulnerable state.

I think we recognize that well we don't have the lion's share of critical minerals here in this country, we do have very good supplies, we certainly have very strong supplies in my home State and an opportunity to gain access to them we're looking at it very critically.

The problem though then the concern is we would have to ship it to China to be processed. So, once again they have the leverage that I think we're trying to get around here. So I appreciate again you highlighting that aspect of what we need to do when we're talking about the supply chain.

I mentioned that we have reintroduced this bill with the proposals that I had outlined in my legislation along with Senator Udall's. A little over 2 years ago at a hearing very similar to what we're having today I asserted that the problem that we have on our hands is very real. Today I would assert that that problem has not diminished.

Our mineral related policies remain outdated, our dependence on foreign minerals is reportedly deepening as you had mentioned. Our agencies are not as coordinated and focused on this issue as I believe they need to be, and when it comes to permitting delays for mines, our Nation is tied for last. In other words we're the worst in the world when it comes to permitting delays.

All along the supply chain our mineral related capabilities have slipped. Unless we take meaningful action, and soon, I think our economy and our security can be jeopardized. Our recent experience with helium shows how dire a shortage of a critical mineral would be for many different industries. We need to realize that unless we do more to ensure our own domestic supply, we may have no way to present—prevent a crisis next time around.

Now our colleagues over in the house have presented ideas to fix this problem and I think that we should consider them fairly just as we expect that they will consider ours. The fact to the matter is that we've taken different approaches between the 2 bodies.

Here in the Senate we focus on the entire supply chain by establishing a process through which minerals can be designated as critical; by adding accountability to the permitting process; by returning agencies to the important work of geological surveying; by seeking alternatives and encouraging recycling; and by promoting a work force that can rise to the challenges that undoubtedly lie ahead.

Now I know that we're all focused here today on the big speech that's going to be delivered in the Capital later this evening. While I would love it, as we are sitting there listening to the President, if he would look at us, Senator Udall, the chairman here, myself and other members of the Energy Committee, and say the State of the Union would be better if we improved our mineral policies.

Now I'm not going to hold my breath for that. Maybe we should try to send some mental telepathy between here and now and then, but I somehow doubt that that's made it into his final text. But it is the truth and these are issues that deserve our attention.

Minerals are the building blocks of our economy, critical to our prosperity, our standard of living and our competitiveness. We need a steady, affordable, and domestic supply of them and as you have pointed out Mr. Chairman, minerals that are mined here, refined here, and processed here, and made into products here.

So again I'm pleased because we've got a good bipartisan bill, it's practical, it's physically responsible, it takes a comprehensive approach to an increasingly complex set of challenges. I think it's worthy of our committee's support and I would hope that we will reach that point very soon.

I'll look forward to the testimony from both panelists and thank you all for agreeing to be here this morning.

The CHAIRMAN. Senator Murkowski thank you for an excellent statement.

I also note that I hope that the bipartisanship of the Senate bill will infiltrate into the other body because their bill was not largely bipartisan. I think it was overwhelmingly a partisan vote. So the good work that you have helped to make possible I hope is going to set off a little bit of a push for some bipartisanship in the house and I thank you for it.

Senator Udall, as Senator Murkowski has said—has put an exceptional amount of time into this and understands this issue inside out, inside and out.

Senator Udall, we welcome you——

Senator UDALL. Thank——

The CHAIRMAN. Please go ahead.

STATEMENT OF HON. MARK UDALL, U.S. SENATOR FROM COLORADO

Senator UDALL. Thank you Mr. Chairman, thank you Senator Murkowski for the kind words and we have been involved in this together. It's been a labor of love, I'm really pleased with the point that we're at and I think we've learned a lot in the process.

One of the things I've learned is that rare earth materials and minerals aren't actually rare they're just rare in concentrated forms. It's very—it's time consuming, it's technologically challenging, although we're going to hear about some of the real advances today to concentrate those minerals and metals.

I think this new term we're using which is critical materials really does the job and sets up the agenda for us and the challenge but also the opportunity. So I want to associate myself with your remarks, both of your remarks and thank you for the kind words.

I have 2 Coloradans I'm going to introduce to you in a minute, but I did want to add a couple of other comments. The reason I got involved in this, this is a very important issue for Colorado and it fits with 2 of my priorities which have been national security and clean energy, that doesn't mean that traditional energy actually needs to use these kinds of materials as well. We ought to be leaders in this area not followers, we can partner with some of the other countries, but we can lead and this is what this legislation really gives us an opportunity to do.

You all mentioned the legislative vehicles you've used, in 2011, I introduced the Critical Minerals and Materials Promotion Act and it focused on the very challenge and opportunity we're talking about here today. My focus was on research and development which would then develop a -or strengthen I should say our domestic supply chain and then would have the result of further developing in more robust critical minerals industry work force.

We want people to know how to do this and I'm really pleased that our revised version, the Critical Minerals Policy Act of 2013, includes these ideas and many more from my legislation as well as from what you all did.

I can't stay for the entire hearing, I hope you'll understand that, but I did want to introduce these 2 Coloradans I mentioned.

I want to start with Dr. Rod Eggert, he's a professor and director of the Division of Economics and Business at the Colorado School of Mines. We're very proud of the Colorado School of Mines.

I don't know, Dr. Eggert, maybe you can speak to this in your comments, But I don't know if there's any other institution in any other state that equals mines, but of course I'm a hometown boy and I care about Mines, it's a wonderful school. As well as our Denver Broncos we're going to win on Sunday, but anyway that—I shouldn't.

[Laughter.]

Senator UDALL. Dr. Eggert you're known as a leading expert on rare earth minerals and you chair the National Research Council and you helped literally to write the book on why critical minerals are so vital to our economy. You're also the deputy director of the Critical Minerals Institute. The Institute is a DOE energy innovation hub and I believe you focus there on research to more efficiently use current materials, reduce waste during manufacturing, diversify our supply and many other important areas of research occur at the institute.

So thank you for that great work and I know the committee will benefit from your expertise.

Sitting just behind you is Jim Sims and he's the Vice President of Corporate Communications for Molycorp. Molycorp is a Colorado based company, it's a world leader in rare earths and rare metals. They have a facility in California, Mountain Pass facility and there—and I just got an update from Jim, Molycorp is creating one of the most energy efficient environmentally friendly rare earth production facilities in the world.

Mr. Chairman, Ranking Member we also have a third witness with us who has a connection with the great State of Colorado and that's Major General Robert Latiff. He was the commander of NORAD, outside Colorado Springs and I'm glad that he's here and able to share some of his insights with the committee today from a national security perspective.

So again thank you all for taking your valuable time. This is a crucial hearing and again I extend my gratitude to the ranking member and the chairman for having this important hearing today. We'll, whip the House of Representatives into shape on this, I have no doubt.

The CHAIRMAN. There you are. Thank you again for the good work you've done, let's just make sure the record is clear, if Senator Cantwell of Washington comes in we are going to give her equal time——

[Laughter.]

The CHAIRMAN [continuing]. To address the gridiron front.

Senator UDALL. That's true.

The CHAIRMAN. Let's go right to our witnesses, we've got Dr. David Danielson the Assistant Secretary for the Office of Energy Efficiency and Renewable Energy at the Department. They house the Critical Minerals Institute and the advanced manufacturing office.

Dr. Larry Meinert, he is the mineral resources program coordinator for the USGS at the Department of the Interior.

Gentleman we will make your prepared remarks a part of the record in their entirety. I've come to feel that there's almost a physiological need at these sessions to read every bit of what we'll put into the record. If you can just kind of summarize your key views, that'll leave plenty of time for questions.

Why don't we start with you Dr. Danielson?

STATEMENT OF DAVID DANIELSON, PH.D., ASSISTANT SECRETARY, OFFICE OF ENERGY EFFICIENCY AND RENEWABLE ENERGY, DEPARTMENT OF ENERGY

Mr. DANIELSON. Great, thank you.

Chairman Wyden, Ranking Member Murkowski, and members of the committee, thank you for the opportunity to testify today on the important role that critical minerals play in moving the U.S. toward a clean energy economy and the Department of Energy's ongoing work related to this topic.

The Department is currently reviewing S. 1600, the Critical Minerals Policy Act of 2013 and has no specific comments on legislation at this time. However DOE strongly believes in the importance of ensuring a stable sustainable domestic supply of critical minerals and has already begun to take significant actions to address this challenge.

I represent DOE's Office of Energy Efficiency and Renewable Energy, EERE, which leads DOE's efforts to help build a strong American clean energy economy.

Critical materials are used in many traditional new and emerging energy applications including in lighting, solar photovoltaics, batteries, and wind turbines, and are expected to play an increasingly important role in meeting our national energy environmental and economic goals going forward.

DOE has been moving swiftly on multiple fronts to address critical materials challenges and issued critical materials strategy reports in 2010 and 2011 that formally identified 5 rare earth materials, dysprosium, neodymium, europium, terbium, and yttrium as critical materials for clean energy applications and identified 2 additional elements lithium and tellurium as near critical materials.

DOE's Critical Materials Strategy Report identified 3 key pillars to address critical materials challenges.

One, diversifying the supply of critical materials, 2, developing substitutes for critical materials, and 3, driving recycling, reuse, and more efficient use of critical materials.

Several entities within DOE contribute to our critical materials R&D effort including the Office of Science, the Advanced Research Projects Agency-Energy, and our applied technology offices including my office EERE.

EERE's R&D investments including its Critical Materials Institute are directly aligned with the aforementioned 3 pillars of DOE's critical materials strategy and are closely coordinated with other efforts across all of DOE.

Regarding the first pillar diversifying supply, EERE has invested in technologies to improve domestic lithium production to supply the domestic battery industry as well as in technologies to recycle lithium batteries. We've also funded the development of technologies to cost effectively extract minerals such as lithium from geothermal brines to improve domestic production of geothermal energy at reduced cost. This year EERE intends to expand this work to develop technologies to cost effectively extract rare earth elements from geothermal brines as well.

In the second pillar the area of critical materials substitutes. DOE has made significant research investments in alternative motor and generator topologies which contain no rare earth permanent magnets at all. EERE has also invested in magnetic materials research to develop magnets with lower rare earth content and to develop completely rare earth free permanent magnets as well. EERE also supports research on next generation wind turbine drive train technologies that could help reduce the use of rare earth elements while continuing to drive down the cost of wind energy.

Improving the recycling and reuse of critical materials in the third pillar has had limited R&D investment at DOE until we recently stood up our Critical Materials Institute, or CMI, in the middle of last year in 2013. Led by Ames National Laboratory, the

Critical Materials Institute which is one of DOE's energy innovation hubs brings together leading researchers from academia national laboratories in the private sector to develop solutions to the domestic shortages of rare earth metals and other materials critical for U.S. energy security.

This institute has focused its R&D efforts around the 3 pillars of the DOE critical materials strategy. For example CMI researchers are studying new lower cost ways to extract, separate, and process rare earth metals from both ores and recycled materials, searching for substitutes for rare earth phosphors for efficient lighting, and developing new high strength, high temperature magnetic materials with low or no rare earth content.

If successful the technologies being developed by CMI could reduce the rare earth content of permanent magnets by more than 50 percent, reduce the amount of critical elements going to domestic landfills in the U.S. by up to 35 percent, and reduce the loss of critical rare earths within domestic manufacturing facilities by up to 50 percent.

Finally DOE would like to underscore the importance of continued interagency coordination and collaboration on the topic of critical materials. DOE co-chairs an interagency subcommittee on critical and strategic mineral supply chains that facilitates coordination across Federal agencies to identify and address important issues related to critical minerals supply issues across all government.

In conclusion the development and implementation of its critical materials strategy including the creation of the Critical Materials Institute, the DOE is taking strong initial steps forward to address the critical materials challenges faced by American manufacturers in the clean energy industry. We look very forward to working with Congress going forward to address the Nation's critical materials challenges.

Thank you.

[The prepared statement of Mr. Danielson follows:]

PREPARED STATEMENT OF DAVID DANIELSON, PH.D., ASSISTANT SECRETARY, OFFICE OF ENERGY EFFICIENCY AND RENEWABLE ENERGY, DEPARTMENT OF ENERGY

Introduction

Chairman Wyden, Ranking Member Murkowski, and Members of the Committee, thank you for the opportunity to testify today on the important role that critical minerals play in moving the U.S. towards a clean energy economy and the U.S. Department of Energy's (DOE) ongoing work related to this topic.

Many domestically-manufactured products rely on critical materials, or materials that are important in their use and subject to supply restrictions. The energy industry is heavily reliant on critical materials and could be significantly affected by supply disruptions and resulting price increases and fluctuations. These critical materials are found in many traditional, new, and emerging energy applications, as well as key ingredients in lighting, solar photovoltaics and batteries, and many other applications. Technologies using critical materials are poised to make even more significant contributions to national energy, environmental, and economic goals.

The Department is currently reviewing S. 1600, the Critical Minerals Policy Act of 2013, and has no specific comments on the legislation at this time. However, the Department believes in the importance of ensuring a stable, sustainable, domestic supply of critical minerals. We look forward to continuing our discussions with Congress on ways to: monitor and identify critical materials as they potentially impact the energy economy; address the production, use, and recycling of critical minerals throughout the supply chain; as well as develop alternatives to critical minerals moving forward.

The Department has been moving swiftly on multiple fronts to address challenges across the lifecycle of critical elements, while also exploring alternatives to those that are hardest to obtain. These efforts are informed by the Department's Critical Materials Strategy developed in 2010 and 2011, which I will be happy to discuss with you today. I will also describe the Critical Materials Institute, an Energy Innovation Hub established by my office last year, and devoted to finding solutions in response to the scarcity of these elements that are critical to U.S. manufacturing and the expansion of clean energy technologies.

DOE is pursuing an all-of-the-above approach to developing every source of American energy. I represent the Office of Energy Efficiency and Renewable Energy (EERE), which leads DOE's efforts to help build a strong clean energy economy, a strategy that is aimed at reducing our reliance on foreign oil, saving families and businesses money, creating jobs, and reducing pollution. We support some of America's best innovators and businesses to research, develop, and demonstrate cutting-edge technologies, and work to break down market barriers in the EERE portfolio's three sectors: 1) sustainable transportation (vehicles, biofuels, hydrogen and fuel cells); 2) energy efficiency (energy-saving homes, buildings, and manufacturing); and 3) renewable electricity generation (solar, geothermal, hydrogen and fuel cells, wind and water).

Our nation stands at a critical point in time regarding the competitive opportunity for clean energy. In 2013, $254 billion was invested globally in clean energy, just over 360 percent increase since 2004; trillions more will be invested in the years ahead.[1] In the decades-long transition to a clean energy economy, the United States faces a stark choice: the clean energy technologies of today and tomorrow can be invented and manufactured in America, or we can surrender global leadership and import these technologies from other countries.

DOE's Critical Materials Strategy

Many of today's clean energy technologies rely on the use of materials with certain essential properties, such as efficient light emission or strong magnetism. Many of those critical materials are essential to producing products that EERE is also investing in, and in order to address this reliance, in both 2010 and 2011, DOE issued Critical Materials Strategy reports that defined and assessed critical materials by analyzing two dimensions: importance to the clean energy industry, and supply risk. The Department's 2010 and 2011 Critical Materials Strategy reports identified five rare earth materials—neodymium, europium, terbium, dysprosium, and yttrium—as critical materials currently essential for America's transition to cost-competitive clean energy technologies, like wind turbines, electric vehicles, and energy efficient lighting. The Strategy reports also identified two additional elements, lithium and tellurium, as "near-critical" materials. Identifying and addressing near-critical element challenges is crucial as both the clean energy industry and critical materials market dynamics change. These particular non-rare earth materials play, at this time, an indispensable role in batteries for hybrid and electric vehicles and commercial photovoltaic thin films, and represent the next-highest criticality in terms of importance to the clean energy industry and risk of supply disruption.

The Department's Critical Materials Strategy reports identified three pillars to address critical materials challenges: 1) diversifying supply of critical materials, 2) developing alternatives to critical materials, and 3) driving recycling, reuse, and more efficient use of critical materials. I will address these in turn: First, diversified global supply chains are essential. To manage supply risk, multiple sources of materials are required. This means taking steps to facilitate the extraction, processing, and manufacturing of critical materials here in the United States, as well as encouraging other nations to expedite alternative supplies. In all cases, extraction, separation, processing, and manufacturing must be done in an environmentally sound manner. Second, substitutes must be developed. Research leading to material and technology substitutes will improve flexibility, decrease demand for critical materials, and help meet the materials needs of the clean energy economy. Third, recycling, reuse and more efficient use of critical materials could significantly lower world demand for newly extracted materials. Research into recycling processes coupled with well-designed policies will help make recycling economically viable over time. Addressing these three pillars is a moving target, as critical materials challenges change over time. Ongoing assessments are necessary to identify the status of current and emerging critical materials; as new technology develops and markets respond to supply risk, the criticality of materials will also shift.

---

[1] See: Bloomberg, "Global Trends in Renewable Energy Investment, Fact Pack as of Q4 2013" (Jan. 2014): http://about.bnef.com/files/2014/01/BNEF_PR_FactPack_Q4_CleanEnergyInvestment_2014-01-15.pdf

DOE R&D Organizations

Several entities within the Department contribute to the critical materials research and development (R&D) effort. The Basic Energy Sciences program in the Office of Science supports broad-based, fundamental materials research. The Advanced Research Projects Agency—Energy (ARPA-E) invests in high-potential, high-impact energy technologies that are likely too early for private-sector investment. Within EERE, investment in research related to critical materials occurs within the Vehicle Technologies Office (VTO), the Wind Power Technologies Office, the Solar Energy Technologies Office (SETO), the Geothermal Technologies Office (GTO), and the Advanced Manufacturing Office (AMO).

DOE national laboratories are also integral to this R&D effort. The national laboratory system includes the nation's historic leader in rare earth materials research, the Ames Laboratory in Ames, Iowa. While Ames Laboratory has a core-competency in rare earth materials, many other national laboratories also contribute significantly to R&D aimed at reducing the criticality of critical materials. For example, Argonne National Laboratory, Brookhaven National Laboratory, Pacific Northwest National Laboratory, Sandia National Laboratories, and Lawrence Berkeley National Laboratory have complementary efforts spanning from basic and applied research to development and demonstration.

In response to the Critical Materials Strategy reports, the Department of Energy launched a national competition for an Energy Innovation Hub. Early in 2013, DOE announced the Critical Materials Institute (CMI), led by Ames National Laboratory. CMI is the nation's premier research, development and analysis institute dedicated to finding innovative solutions and developing creative, transformational paths to eliminating the criticality of rare earth and other materials. CMI began operations in June of 2013. CMI has brought together leading researchers from academia, four Department of Energy national laboratories, as well as the private sector to develop solutions to the domestic shortages of rare earth metals and other materials critical for U.S. energy security. CMI addresses materials criticality problems by developing technologies spanning the supply chain for the rare earth (plus lithium and tellurium) elements, as well as providing research infrastructure to address any emergent challenges related to materials criticality.

CMI faces a formidable task: developing solutions to potential supply chain risks across the lifecycle of several different materials. The solutions will not be the same for different kinds of materials or applications. For example, technologies to improve separation and processing of rare earth elements from domestic deposits may increase the supply of neodymium (for magnets) but not europium (for lighting) due to the ore composition.

The Institute has focused its efforts around the three pillars of the Critical Materials Strategy. For example, to diversify supply, researchers are studying new, lower cost ways to extract, separate and process rare earth metals from ores and recycled materials. To develop substitutes, Institute researchers, in partnership with private sector partners, are searching for substitutes for rare earth phosphors. Energy-efficient lighting phosphors currently need europium, terbium, and yttrium, and this group is searching for alternatives using materials such as manganese. To improve reuse and recycling, CMI's R&D in this area is focused on two major areas: first, improving the cost- and energy-efficiency of separating the rare earth containing components from end-of-life products like light bulbs, hard drives and motors; and second, developing new technologies to extract rare earth elements from these end-of-life components to produce new materials. If successful, the technologies proposed by CMI could reduce loss of critical rare earths within domestic manufacturing by 50 percent and reduce critical rare earths elements going to domestic landfills by 35 percent.

In its first year of operations, the team is off to a fast start. Key start-up and management operations have been put in place. About 35 projects across the Institute are up and running. All of these projects involve multiple partners, often three or four partners collaborating to achieve the best solutions under CMI's mission. EERE is pleased to report that CMI researchers filed seven intellectual property invention disclosures. While there is tremendous work still to be done by the Institute, that is a great sign of things to come.

R&D Progress by DOE Programs

In my office and across the Department, we have an obligation to research issues relevant to supporting manufacturing as it relates to energy. Increasing U.S. manufacturing competiveness relies on thinking broadly about addressing challenges across the supply chain and across various industrial applications in our R&D investments. By stepping up research related to critical materials, DOE will help ensure clean energy technologies will be invented and manufactured in America.

EERE's R&D investments are directly aligned with the aforementioned three pillars of the Critical Materials Strategy and coordinated among the program offices across the Department.

Regarding the first pillar—diversifying supply—some of the key research challenges in separations and processing of rare earth elements have been addressed historically at a small scale within the research portfolios of the Basic Energy Sciences program in the Office of Science, Laboratory Directed Research and Development, Small Business Innovation Research, and Small Business Technology Transfer. EERE has also invested in technologies to improve domestic lithium production. Through the American Recovery and Reinvestment Act of 2009, VTO supported a project to expand lithium carbonate and lithium hydroxide production to supply the domestic battery industry as well as a project to recycle lithium batteries for resale of lithium carbonate. The EERE Geothermal Technologies Office has funded the development of technologies to cost effectively extract minerals such as lithium, manganese and zinc from geothermal brines—to improve domestic production at reduced costs and to increase the overall value of geothermal electricity generation.

For substitutes, DOE has made significant investments, specifically toward rare earth permanent magnets for motors and generators. For instance, both EERE (through VTO and the Wind Power Technologies Office) and ARPA-E have significant efforts related to addressing rare earth materials criticality in these areas through the development of alternative motor and generator topologies which do not require rare earth permanent magnets. VTO has also invested in optimizing the use of rare earth materials in permanent magnets—focusing on magnet processing, composition, and improving high temperature performance with reduced rare earth content. In addition, VTO supported researchers are working to develop rare earth-free permanent magnets for advanced traction motors. For example, they are modifying aluminum, nickel and cobalt (alnico) magnets for improved performance in these new motors and developing new iron-cobalt based alloys to replace rare earth permanent magnets. ARPA-E's "Rare Earth Alternatives in Critical Technologies" program focuses on early-stage alternative technologies that reduce or eliminate the need for rare earths by developing substitutes in two key areas: electric vehicle motors and wind generators. Technological advances that utilize low-cost and abundant alternatives such as manganese and nickel will become increasingly vital to our national economic and energy security. The projects funded by ARPA-E must aim to meet or exceed the performance of their rare earth predecessors while remaining cost-competitive.

EERE's Wind Power Technologies Office supports several next-generation drive train technology projects. One of the key goals for these projects is reduction in the cost of wind energy. Although not a stated requirement for the program, many of these innovative technologies would also reduce or eliminate the use of permanent magnets containing rare earth materials, particularly for next-generation direct-drive wind turbines. For example, innovative superconducting direct-drive generators and new processes to make these materials on a cost-competitive basis for large wind turbines are being investigated.

The Department is also addressing substitutes for near-critical materials. DOE's 2011 Critical Materials Strategy classified lithium as "near-critical." R&D efforts continue across the Department to develop alternatives to this material. In December 2012, the Joint Center for Energy Storage Research (JCESR), which is the Energy Innovation Hub for Battery and Energy Storage, began operations. JCESR is managed out of DOE's Office of Science and is led by Argonne National Laboratory. The mission of JCESR is to develop new battery chemistries beyond lithium-ion, and its goal is to deliver electrical energy storage with less or no lithium, five times the energy density, and at one-fifth the cost of today's commercial batteries within five years.

Additionally, in the 2011 Critical Materials Strategy, tellurium was also assessed as near-critical. It is a material used in solar cells being deployed in the United States today. EERE's Solar Energy Technologies Office has supported a large number of projects to develop new technologies that focus on earth abundant materials as alternate, inexpensive materials in solar photovoltaics. For example, in September 2011, DOE awarded funding to 23 projects ($24.5 million) through the Next Generation Photovoltaics II solicitation, many of which incorporated earth-abundant materials such as copper, iron, and tin. Improving the recycling and reuse of critical materials—the third pillar—has, until recently, had limited DOE R&D investment. However, with the startup of the Critical Materials Institute and its work in this area, DOE is primed to make strides in this arena of R&D.

Interagency Coordination

Finally, the Department would also like to underscore the importance of continued interagency coordination and collaboration on the topic of critical materials. Issues related to critical materials and minerals touch on the missions of many federal agencies, and the full interagency perspective can help us proactively address critical materials issues. DOE co-chairs the National Science and Technology Council's Subcommittee on Critical and Strategic Mineral Supply Chains, which was established in December 2010. This Subcommittee facilitates a strong, coordinated effort across federal agencies to identify and address important policy implications arising from strategic minerals supply issues. Areas of focus for the Subcommittee include identifying emerging critical materials, improving depth of information, and identifying R&D priorities. The Subcommittee also informally reviews and examines domestic and global policies that affect the supply of critical materials, such as permitting, export restrictions, recycling, and stockpiling.

Conclusion

The work being done across the Department, including at the Critical Materials Institute, shows that DOE is taking steps to address the global demand for critical materials that underpin clean energy technologies. The United States intends to be a world leader in clean energy technologies. To this end, we must ensure a sustainable domestic supply chain for our clean energy economy. We look forward to working with Congress on addressing critical materials challenges.

The CHAIRMAN. Thank you.

Mr. MEINERT.

STATEMENT OF LAWRENCE D. MEINERT, MINERAL RESOURCES PROGRAM COORDINATOR, U.S. GEOLOGICAL SURVEY, DEPARTMENT OF THE INTERIOR

Mr. MEINERT. Good morning Chairman Wyden, ranking member—Good morning Chairman Wyden, Ranking Member Murkowski and members of the committee, and thank you for the opportunity to discuss the Critical Minerals Policy Act of 2013, I'm joined today by Karen Mouritsen, deputy assistant director energy minerals and realty management for the Bureau of Land Management.

The Department of the Interior supports the goal of facilitating the development of critical minerals in an environmentally responsible manner. As background the U.S. Geological Survey is responsible for conducting research and collecting data on a wide variety of mineral resources. Studies include how and where deposits are formed, the interactions of minerals with the environment, and information to document current production and consumption of about 100 mineral commodities within the United States and around the world.

This full spectrum of mineral resource science allows for comprehensive understanding of the complete life cycle of mineral resources and materials including resource formation, discovery, production, consumption, use, recycling, and reuse, and allows for understanding of environmental issues of concern throughout the lifecycle.

The Bureau of Land Management administers over 245 million surface acres of public land located in the 12 Western States including Alaska, as well as 700 million acres of subsurface mineral estate throughout the Nation. The BLM manages mineral development under a number of different authorities. Each of these authorities along with the BLM regulations and guidance provides a legal framework for the development of minerals including critical minerals on Federal and Indian lands.

Global demand for critical mineral commodity is on the rise with increasing applications of consumer products, computers, automobiles, aircraft, and other advanced technology products. To better understand potential sources of critical mineral commodities the USGS has completed studies of known domestic and global rare earth reserves, resources, and uses, which summarize basic geologic facts and materials flow issues related to rare earth element resources one type of critical materials.

Other USGS studies analyze worldwide trade and supply chains for other critical minerals including lithium, platinum group metals, and tantalum.

In 2012 the United States was 100 percent dependent on foreign suppliers for 17 mineral commodities and more than 50 percent dependent on mineral sources for an additional 24 mineral commodities.

In 2008 a National Research Council Committee funded largely by the USGS, developed a criticality matrix that combines supply risk with importance of use as a first step toward determining which mineral commodities are essential to the Nation's economic and national security.

This has been updated by subsequent studies and ongoing work by the Critical and Strategic Mineral Supply Chain Interagency Subcommittee of the National Science and Technology Council. As David mentioned that is co-chaired by DOE and the USGS representing the Department of the Interior.

For S. 1600 it directs the Secretary of the Interior through the Director of the USGS to perform a number of actions that build on current USGS activities and capabilities, including the recent rare earth element inventory that I mentioned. It also describes the BLM -directs the BLM to improve the quality and timeliness of decisions regarding the environmentally responsible development of critical minerals on Federal lands. The BLM supports the responsible development of minerals on Federal lands and is working to improve efficiencies while ensuring protection of other resources.

In conclusion the Department maintains a work force of geoscientists including geologist, geochemist, geophysicists, and resource specialists with expertise on critical minerals and materials. The Department continuously collects, analyzes and disseminates dated information on domestic and global rare earth and other critical mineral reserves and resources, production, consumption, and use.

The Department through the USGS stands ready to fulfill its role as the Federal provider of unbiased research on known mineral resources, assessment of undiscovered mineral resources, and information on domestic and global production and consumption of mineral resources for use in global critical mineral supply chain analysis.

The BLM is committed to implementing efficiencies for the environmentally responsible development of critical minerals on Federal lands.

Thank you for the opportunity to present the views of the Department on S. 1600, I'll be happy to answer any questions.

[The prepared statement of Mr. Meinert follows:]

PREPARED STATEMENT OF LAWRENCE D. MEINERT, MINERAL RESOURCES PROGRAM COORDINATOR, U.S. GEOLOGICAL SURVEY, DEPARTMENT OF THE INTERIOR

Good morning Chairman Wyden, Ranking Member Murkowski, and Members of the Committee, and thank you for the opportunity to discuss S. 1600, the Critical Minerals Policy Act of 2013. The bill directs the Secretaries of the Interior and Energy to perform a large number of activities intended to support and enhance the Nation's critical mineral supply chain, beginning with developing a methodology to determine which minerals are critical to the Nation's economy. In this statement, I will address the provisions relevant to the Department of the Interior.

The Department of the Interior supports the goal of facilitating the development of critical minerals in an environmentally responsible manner. We note that many of the activities called for in S. 1600 are within the scope of existing Department of the Interior authorities.

Background

The U.S. Geological Survey (USGS) is responsible for conducting research and collecting data on a wide variety of mineral resources. Research is conducted to understand the geologic processes that have concentrated known mineral resources at specific localities in the Earth's crust and to estimate (or assess) quantities, qualities, and areas of undiscovered mineral resources, or potential future supply. USGS scientists also conduct research on the interactions of mineral resources with the environment, both natural and as a result of resource extraction, to better predict the degree of impact that resource development may have on human and ecosystem health. USGS mineral commodity specialists collect, analyze, and disseminate data and information that document current production and consumption for about 100 mineral commodities, both domestically and internationally for 180 countries. This full spectrum of mineral resource science allows for a comprehensive understanding of the complete life cycle of mineral resources and materials-resource formation, discovery, production, consumption, use, recycling, and reuse-and allows for an understanding of environmental issues of concern throughout the life cycle.

Global demand for critical mineral commodities is on the rise with increasing applications in consumer products, computers, automobiles, aircraft, and other advanced technology products. Much of this demand growth is driven by new technologies that increase energy efficiency and decrease reliance on fossil fuels. To better understand potential sources of critical mineral commodities, the USGS has completed studies of known domestic and global rare-earth reserves, resources, and uses (Long and others, 2010; Tse, 2011; Wilburn, 2012). These studies summarize basic geologic facts and materials flow issues related to rare earth element resources, which are a type of critical mineral. Other USGS studies analyze world trade and supply chains for other critical minerals including lithium, platinum-group metals, and tantalum (Goonan, 2012; Yager and others, 2012; Soto-Viruet and others, 2013).

The Bureau of Land Management (BLM) administers over 245 million surface acres of public land located in the 12 Western states, including Alaska, as well as 700 million acres of sub-surface mineral estate throughout the nation. The BLM manages mineral development under a number of different authorities, including the Federal Land Policy and Management Act, the Mineral Leasing Act of 1920, the Materials Act of 1947, and the Mining Law of 1872. Each of these authorities, along with BLM regulations and guidance, provides a legal framework for the development of minerals, including critical minerals, on Federal and Indian lands.

Though rare earth elements are currently of most concern to many stakeholders, including the Department of Defense which funded some of the studies, it should be noted that in 2012 the United States was 100 percent dependent on foreign suppliers for 17 mineral commodities and more than 50 percent dependent on foreign sources for an additional 24 mineral commodities. Import partners include Brazil, Canada, China, France, Germany, Japan, Mexico, Russia, and Venezuela. In 2008, a National Research Council committee, funded largely by the USGS, developed a "criticality matrix" that combines supply risk with importance of use as a first step toward determining which mineral commodities are essential to the Nation's economic and national security (National Research Council, 2008). This has been updated by subsequent studies and ongoing work by the Critical and Strategic Mineral Supply Chain Interagency sub-committee of the National Science and Technology Council, which is co-chaired by the USGS on behalf of the Department of the Interior.

S. 1600

S. 1600, the Critical Minerals Policy Act of 2013, directs the Secretary of the Interior, through the Director of the USGS, to perform a number of actions that build on current USGS activities and capabilities, including the recent rare earths inventory. The bill in Section 101 directs the USGS to develop a rigorous methodology for determining which minerals are critical and then to use that methodology to designate critical minerals. Section 103 calls for a comprehensive national mineral resource assessment within four years of the bill's enactment for each mineral designated as critical under Sec. 101, and it authorizes field work for the assessment, as well as technical and financial assistance for States and Indian tribes. The bill establishes in Section 108 a collaborative effort between USGS, academic institutions, and the U.S. Energy Information Administration for annual reviews of domestic critical mineral trends as well as forward-looking analyses of critical mineral production, consumption, and recycling patterns. Section 301 of the bill repeals the National Critical Minerals Act of 1984.

S. 1600, Section 102, amends the National Materials and Minerals Policy, Research and Development Act of 1980 to encourage Federal agencies to facilitate the availability, development and environmentally-responsible production of critical minerals. Section 105 directs the BLM to improve the quality and timeliness of decisions regarding the environmentally responsible development of critical minerals on Federal lands. The BLM supports the responsible development of minerals on Federal lands and is working to improve efficiencies while ensuring protection of other resources. Section 105 also directs the BLM to annually report on the implementation of these measures and on critical and hardrock mineral production on Federal land. We note that under the Mining Law of 1872, the BLM does not collect the quantity, type, and estimated value of minerals produced on Federal land.

Conclusion

The Department maintains a workforce of geoscientists (geologists, geochemists, geophysicists, and resource specialists) with expertise in critical minerals and materials. The Department continuously collects, analyzes, and disseminates data and information on domestic and global rare-earth and other critical mineral reserves and resources, production, consumption, and use. This information is published annually in the USGS Mineral Commodity Summaries (USGS, 2013) and includes a description of current events, trends, and issues related to supply and demand.

The Department, through the USGS, stands ready to fulfill its role as the federal provider of unbiased research on known mineral resources, assessment of undiscovered mineral resources, and information on domestic and global production and consumption of mineral resources for use in global critical mineral supply chain analysis. The BLM is committed to implementing efficiencies for the environmentally-responsible development of critical minerals on Federal lands.

We note, however, that many of the activities called for in S. 1600 are already authorized by existing authorities. Any activities conducted to fulfill the objectives of the bill would require substantial resources and would need to compete for funding with other priorities.

Thank you for the opportunity to present the views of the Department on S. 1600. I will be happy to answer any questions.

The CHAIRMAN. Alright gentlemen, thank you very much.

Dr. Danielson let me start with you.

We've talked about how the supply of critical minerals is essential for a whole host of things; let's start with say—electric vehicles. It seems to me this is also an opportunity though to significantly improve the economics of a number of other energy technologies. So for example minerals like lithium can be recovered from battery packs now one of the major costs of electric vehicles. So we tried to capture as many of these opportunities as we could.

You have a background in materials science, what additional recommendations might you have so that we can continue with our work on minerals to recapture as much economic value as we possibly can? That's why I cited the example of the lithium recovery from the battery pack. Are there are other areas where we can recapture value?

Mr. DANIELSON. Thank you for that question Mr. Chairman.

You know DOE performed these—the Critical Materials Strategy Reports in 2010 and updated it in 2011 and our approach was really based on the 3 pillars I mentioned. You know the first being diversifying supply, the second being about developing substitutes that don't have criticality, and the third is really focused on reuse and recycling and more efficient use of critical materials. The third pillar is really the area that you're touching upon.

I think we've seen tremendous opportunities on the recycling side in a number of critical technologies as you mentioned. For DOE's work we've identified 4 specific technologies that are especially vulnerable to critical materials, electric vehicles both for motors, permanent magnets for motors and lithium for batteries, efficient phosphors for lighting where europium, terbium, yttrium are critical there. Wind turbines, which is an area where permanent magnets are a big part of the road map going forward which contain critical materials.

One of the areas where we see great opportunity and we're attacking this head on with the Critical Materials Institute is in the area of recycling rare earth phosphors from fluorescent light bulbs. This is an area where europium, terbium, yttrium, they're—these are critical elements that we've identified, 3 of 5 critical elements at DOE. We're already collecting about 30 percent of fluorescent light bulbs to remove the mercury from these light bulbs.

So we already have a supply chain to collect those materials, but we don't have the cost effective technology to separate out the rare earths from those phosphors. So one of the major focus areas of our institute is in developing new separations technologies which is an area where we haven't made a lot of investment in the past but I already see a lot of opportunity to cost effectively recycle those rare earth elements in phosphors.

The CHAIRMAN. Good let me ask you one other question.

One of the things I was struck by with respect to this issue, when I talked to Senator Murkowski and Senator Udall who have spent so much time on it, is that the programs that the Department-that the Federal Government really runs were just sort of strewn all over the country side. There are a lot of different programs and just because you have a lot of people in the kitchen doesn't necessarily mean you produce a good meal.

[Laughter.]

The CHAIRMAN. You've worked in materials science for quite some time. Is it your view that making sure that we have a more organized effort here, which is right at the heart of the bill, is a valuable contribution that this legislation makes?

Mr. DANIELSON. Yes, without commenting directly on the bill itself I would point out that——

The CHAIRMAN. We know the people at OMB are listening, I just want to make sure that the emphasis of the sponsors, which is to have a more organized effort that the value of that is something that you and other experts realize.

Mr. DANIELSON. Yes, I and my colleagues, we see tremendous value in having coherent efforts around this, and within the Department as well as across all of government we have seen that within the DOE universe it was tremendously valuable to have our energy policy and strategic analysis office take the lead in organizing all of us. As my colleague mentioned we have an interagency subcommittee on critical and strategic mineral supply chains where we are all pulling together and so we—I see tremendous value in interagency——

The CHAIRMAN. Let me use——

Mr. DANIELSON [continuing]. Coordination.

The CHAIRMAN. Let me use my last 20 seconds on something that's important for folks at home, at Oregon State.

On December 20th a senior official in your office informed the directors of the Northwest National Marine Renewable Energy Center, which has collaboration between Oregon State University and University of Washington, that it would not be receiving any more funding to operate. It's our view that this is a critical area. We're falling behind our international competitors.

It's my understanding that the Senators funding agreement with DOE runs through the first half of fiscal 2015 so you're not only cutting them off, but you are cutting them off in mid stream. Also that was a decision made a full month before Congress passed the Appropriations Bill, which provided the funding that we thought was needed to continue the program.

Before the end of the week, I want to hear back from you on why this decision was made and in light of the fact that the Congress has passed and the President has now signed this new bill whether or not continued funding is going to be provided to the center. Will you get back to me on this by the close of business Friday?

Mr. DANIELSON. Absolutely.

The CHAIRMAN. Very good, alright.

Senator MURKOWSKI. Thank you Mr. Chairman and gentleman, I do appreciate you being here, but I have to admit I am a little bit disappointed in the written testimony that you have provided and your comments indirect support or opposition of the bill are very—they're so nuanced I can't tell, which is not usually a good sign.

But—and we've got a second panel here that I think speaks very clearly to some of the issues that have been raised in S. 1600, so I'd like Dr. Danielson for you to give me a little bit more of your comments in—both in writing and what you have affirmed here is the Department is currently reviewing it, you've got no specific comments on the legislation at this time.

We introduced the bill back in late October, we certainly gave plenty of notice to the Department that we were planning this hearing and asking for folks to come in and testify. It's not a lengthy bill it's only 40 pages long. Are you saying that nobody within the Department has really had an opportunity to review and to be able to then provide comment?

Mr. DANIELSON. Critical materials is an area that the Department and our interagency task force takes very seriously. I think we've evidenced that at DOE by publishing these critical materials reports that allow——

Senator MURKOWSKI. Yes, but what about this bill that has been out there now for 3 months, this 40 page bill. If critical minerals are so important why have you not formed an opinion one way or another that you would like to relay publicly?

Mr. DANIELSON. At this point the DOE is reviewing it. We don't have any formal administration comments on the bill itself. I would welcome a request if desired for technical assistance related to this bill to the Department of Energy.

Senator MURKOWSKI. I don't know that there's any technical assistance. I think you guy's just need to read the bill and let us know whether it's something that you can support or not support. Everything that you have conveyed here in the hearing about the significance, the importance of critical minerals in our supply chain is certainly all fine well and good and we're talking about what you're doing within the Department to ensure that we're focusing on recycling, reuse, the other priorities. But we need to move a bill in order to advance some of this so we would greatly appreciate DOE weighing in.

Dr. Meinert your testimony begins by stating that the Department supports the goal of facilitating the development of critical minerals in an environmentally responsible manner, you repeated that a couple of times, do you think that enactment of this bill would further enhance that goal?

Mr. MEINERT. Yes, we have read the bill in detail and we are thrilled and delighted at a bill that focuses on mineral resources. I as the head of the mineral resources program am particularly thrilled and delighted that the bill focuses on this critical need for the Nation. So as I stated very clearly here the Department is supportive of the goals of this bill and we are glad to see it introduced.

Senator MURKOWSKI. I'm thrilled and delighted, thank you.

Let me ask both of you in the bill itself we—where we establish a process to designate which minerals are critical. We require that the list not exceed 20 in total, and I have to confess that that's a somewhat arbitrary number. The question to both of you is whether or not you think we have the right number? Should we be higher, should we be lower, does it make a difference? Your input here, Dr. Meinert you can go first.

Mr. MEINERT. This is a subject that we spent a lot of time on so we are the Nation's chief compiler of this type of information and so we've given a lot of thought to it. As you have pointed out there is no specific number that is absolutely correct.

If you look at the various estimates that have been made around the world, so the European Union has looked at this and came up with a list of 14 elements in their study in 2011 and then they have redone that study and now expanded it beyond 20. So it's very clear that reasonable people could come up with lists of different lengths and I think the actual length of the list is less important than focusing the Nation and the world's attention upon minerals resources as a subject.

So we are comfortable with the number that you have put forward and we recognize that it's not an absolute number and we understand the reasoning behind it.

Senator MURKOWSKI. OK, good, good.

Mr. MEINERT. I'll add that in our DOE—you know detailed DOE critical materials assessment strategy we looked at 16 separate materials that were identified by our stakeholders and narrowed that down to 5 to 7 just within the Department of Energy space. So if we look at our interagency level a number in the—on the order of 20 plus or minus seems like a reasonable number.

Senator MURKOWSKI. OK, thank you Mr. Chairman.

The CHAIRMAN. Thank you Senator Murkowski.

In order of arrival we have Senator Baldwin, Senator Risch, and then Senator Franken.

Senator BALDWIN. Thank you Mr. Chairman, Ranking Member Murkowski.

I'm delighted that we're having this hearing and I wanted to just start off with a couple of points that are slightly off topic for the bill but related. One is that the bill obviously focuses on critical materials critical minerals and you were drilling down on the critical aspect of it. Right now the State of Wisconsin is facing a very severe propane shortage.

Now I'm not pretending that's the subject matter of the bill before us, but it gives a really stark illustration of what happens when there are disruptions, how dangerous it can be when resources that we absolutely rely on for, in this case warmth of our constituents homes are disrupted and we need a stable supply of our critical resources.

The other issue that I wanted to bring up where Wisconsin I think is playing a proud leadership role is also slightly off topic, but pretty closely related and that's the supply of, and I can never pronounce this very accurately, but Molybdenum-99. We nickname it Moly-99, which is used in a lot of health diagnostic applications.

Currently our country is reliant on nondomestic sources for this in reactors in Canada, in the Netherlands, and elsewhere in the world. Because of maintenance and other shutdowns of these reactors we've been in short supply. I think its 55 thousand Americans use or have tests in any given day that use Moly-99 and our domestic production of it is going to be important in the future and Wisconsin is taking a real lead in that in coming up with non-reactor based ways of producing Moly-99.

While not the subject of this legislation it is related closely and an area in which my state is very concerned. I—this bill is important to my state not because we are the home to large or even any perhaps supply or stocks of critical minerals, but we are home to manufacturers that rely on these critical minerals in their products and also as a manufacturing state have long been the home to companies that build the mining machines that extract these minerals.

So this legislation and these policies at the national level are really critical to my State's economy too and I am very appreciative that we're spending some time on this today.

Dr. Danielson, I took particular notice in your written testimony and your testimony provided here today about the value of one of your pillars the recycling and reuse programs for critical minerals and how research into recycling processes could make these more economically viable over time. Wisconsin is home to recycling businesses like Veolia Environmental Services as an example which utilizes innovative ways to remove hazardous materials like mercury from our waste stream.

But recycling programs not only reduce the amount of unwanted waste products they also and crucially can reduce demand for newly extracted critical minerals. So based on the testimony that we've heard today indicating a demand for critical minerals that continues to outpace our domestic supply, recycling programs can be ever more important.

I'm interested in knowing in more detail the strategies that the Department is utilizing to improve the recycling of critical materials and what you view as the greatest opportunities for recycling and reuse in your sphere and energy?

Mr. DANIELSON. Thank you very much Senator for that question.

Recycling is one of the 3 pillars that we really are driving our strategy around, and the Critical Materials Institute being at the center of our strategy. We're looking at a wide array of activities across the whole supply chain, which I think, is one of the key important elements of the approach the bill is taking. All the way from you know separations, processes that can actually remove the small amounts of these rare earths from magnets or phosphors that need to be recycled.

All the way going back to analyzing—designing these motors or batteries or lighting fixtures so that they're easy to disassemble and perform recycling processes on. One of the elements that is particularly critical when it comes to the clean energy applications is dysprosium, which is very important for magnets that can perform at high temperature required, especially, for motors for electric vehicles.

So that element in particular is one that we are targeting in a serious way as we go forward with our work related to recycling of critical materials.

The CHAIRMAN. Thank you Senator Baldwin.

I'm going to recognize Senator Risch, but just note that I'm very pleased that you brought up this propane issue and I know Senator Franken cares a lot about this as well because the Midwest has been hit very hard. Senator Murkowski and I have always tried to make sure that the committee and those who are following these issues can get briefed.

So this afternoon at 3:30 in this room the Energy Information Administration will be putting on a briefing at the request of Senator Murkowski and I—and this is going to be important and I think actually quite fitting this week. Not only are people really getting clobbered with these high propane prices, but it also gets into the issue that we're going to have to debate and that's the question of exports. Senator Murkowski and I have agreed that Thursday we're going to have a hearing on the whole oil export issues.

So we'll have a good briefing this afternoon and on Thursday all who are interested in that issue and I think it's very timely that we have the debate and start talking about the pros and cons and Heaven forbid have a civilized conversation about the merits of an important issue.

We're very glad Senator Risch is here, he's got a lot of expertise in this area.

Senator RISCH. Thank you Mr. Chairman.

Senator Baldwin I was delighted to hear you talk about the issues with Moly–99, there's a lot of us been beating the drum for many years on this. There's absolutely no reason why the United States of America should be reliant on other countries to provide this.

Most Americans have no idea how important it is in the diagnostic aspects of medicine and obviously at the Idaho National Laboratory there's been work done on this and we've been a player in this for a long time, so welcome to the fight and I hope you'll join us.

I think that Moly–99 and all these others are—is underscoring a situation we have in America where as we do more and more of these high tech things we're going to be more reliant on some very rare commodities and last year we went through the helium fight, which again most Americans weren't aware of how critical it is.

We have a very large high tech operation in Idaho called Micron Technology and they are incredibly reliant as is virtually all—are virtually all IT manufacturers on helium and so we got right to the edge I think, but in a bipartisan manner we got the job done and we're going to be hitting more and more of these walls I think as we go forward. So this hearing is particularly important.

Again most people don't realize how many of these critical commodities there are and how reliant we are on countries like China where political stability in the long term certainly is not something that can be counted on and so we need to continue that.

I want to thank the chairman and co-chairman for sending bill S. 1600, I'm proud to be a co-sponsor with many other people. It is very simple, it simply directs the USGS to establish a list of these critical minerals that we need and then set out a comprehensive set of policies, and I'm assuming they would give these policies to us because this is going to be a matter of debate and I think that we should all have or get our 2 cents worth it.

The question I have for the 2 witnesses briefly is these 2 things that were being—were asked the USGS to do is to establish a list of minerals and to set out a comprehensive set of policies. It's something that I'm sure there's been a lot work done on over the years so the question I have for you is how much of this work is already done, that is what kind of an effort is this bill going to take and how quickly can we expect to get some results from this?

Dr. Meinert maybe we could start with you?

Mr. MEINERT. Thank you for that question.

We have indeed done a lot of work on this over the years, some of this is continuing and ongoing work so the inventory of materials, the collection of materials flow, studies of the global trade tracking that—that's something we do on a continuous basis and every year we put out the minerals commodities summary that describes for the Nation and for the world what's the resources are and their availability. So that's one part of the whole criticality analysis is having the data that you would then base those analysis on.

Relative——

Senator RISCH. I'm glad to hear that you've done that much work already I mean that—and that—obviously that's a foundational point that's very critical if we're going to answer these questions so thank you for that.

Mr. MEINERT. We appreciate your support for that because this requires a huge amount of work if you can imagine anybody's who's collected this sort of data. The other part of the bill directs is the assessment of critical materials in the United States and that would be a major, major undertaking. We have done assessments of many different areas we just completed the first global assessment for copper which is the assessment of the entire world for copper.

So we have the expertise, we have the methodology for doing this and we have done a lot of work in development and anticipation of doing these sort of assessments and we try to maintain the scientific capability to perform that service for the Nation.

Senator RISCH. Thanks very much.

Mr. DANIELSON. Thank you, Mr. Senator.

I would just add or reiterate you know that we've done a lot of work to date with the leadership of the Department of the Interior and USGS in particular in establishing methodology that works in terms of criticality assessment and we've applied that to the Department of Energy through our critical materials strategy report and that's been the basis for our work.

I think we are ahead of the curve in terms of we are collaborating across the agencies through this interagency working group on critical and strategic mineral supply chains out of the National Science and Technology Council. But I do believe that there is more work to be done, but I do think we're setup to work together well under the leadership of whatever entity would take the lead going forward.

Senator RISCH. Thank you Mr. Danielson.

Thank you, Mr. Chairman.

The CHAIRMAN. Senator Franken.

Senator FRANKEN. Thank you Mr. Chairman.

I have to run so I'm going to submit my questions for the record.

I would like to say thank you for having this 3:30 meeting on propane. We in Minnesota have had very cold winter, we've had our corn came in kind of wet and we used the propane to dry that, so thank you for having that meeting at 3:30.

One of the things I just want to say is that you know so many of these critical minerals are needed for things like electric cars and for—just for winter binds and lighting and that this—I know that so many folks want to make sure that we are able to do those technologies to lower our carbon footprint and the tradeoff in terms of making sure that we—Mr. Meinert at the Bureau of Land Management you're looking at the environmental aspects of the processes by we—which we get these things. I want to keep a lot of people to understand that these are essential in these clean energy technologies and that's why I'm proud to be a sponsor of the Chairman and Ranking Member's bill.

So I'll submit those questions for the record and thank you gentleman for your testimony, thank you Secretary Danielson for coming to Minnesota so recently.

Thanks.

The CHAIRMAN. Thank you Senator Franken.

I don't have any other questions for this panel, Senator Murkowski any additional questions?

Senator MURKOWSKI. I have just one very quick one for Dr. Meinert and you mentioned the assessment going forward and what I am curious about and would like to understand better is, what's our analytical capacity here in assessing future supply and demand?

As we kind of forecast out and we've got a section in this bill that relates to forecasting, can you tell us whether USGS supports a joint effort with EIA to bolster our analytical and forecasting capabilities for these minerals?

You talked a lot in your—both of you in your opening statements particularly Mr. Danielson here in terms of how we diversify supply, how we look for substitutes, how we recycle, reuse. We know that we're going to continue to do good things in Senator Baldwin's state in terms of manufacturing so we're going to need more, but given the effort that is underway with substitution or reuse, how do we forecast with any degree of reliability?

Mr. Meinert the question is for you, but I think it also goes to what you're doing in DOE as well.

Mr. MEINERT. Forecasting is a complex science and the foundation is always built upon the data that you have and so you are looking at the history, the current uses, the current supplies and then modeling that forward. So we have some experience with that, our main expertise is in the collection of the data, the assessment of the resources.

You mentioned EIA, they certainly have done much more in the modeling realm than we have. But we have a long history of working with other Federal agencies, both DOE, BOM with an Interior, EPA, and a lot of agencies to try to work toward a common goal.

Senator MURKOWSKI. Do you think it makes sense to bring in EIA or others that may have that assessment or forecasting perspective?

Mr. MEINERT. As we move in that direction we would certainly attempt to learn from anybody who has——

Senator MURKOWSKI. Yes.

Mr. MEINERT [continuing]. Been further out in the curve than we are.

Senator MURKOWSKI. Dr. Danielson.

Mr. DANIELSON. I will point out that, although it's not under my purview, I know that the EIA would welcome any partnership that would be beneficial to the USGS to share best practices that have been established at the EIA and have worked out well in terms of forecasting.

Senator MURKOWSKI. OK, thank you Mr. Chairman and I would hope that as we move forward, not only with this legislation, but just in the efforts that are out there, that when we talk about the interagency coordination that that is more than just good buzz words, it's—we all talk about interagency working, but it really is going to be necessary in this area to know and understand what we have and how cross department we can be working to be more effective in all these areas.

With that I thank both of the witnesses and look forward to second panel.

The CHAIRMAN. Alright we'll excuse you, thank you gentlemen.

Our next panel retired Major General Robert Latiff a research professor and director in the Intelligence and National Security Research Center at George Mason University and an adjunct professor at Notre Dame. He previously served as vice commander for the U.S. Air Force Electronics System Center and as commander of the NORAD Cheyenne Mountain Operation Center in Colorado.

Mr. David Isaacs, the vice president of Government Affairs for the Semiconductor Industry Association. Semiconductors are of enormous importance in my home state so we're glad that they're here.

Jennifer Thomas is the director of Federal Government Affairs for the Auto Alliance, a leading advocacy group for the automobile sector and we're very glad that Senator Stabenow felt that it was important to have Mr. Thomas.

Mr. Jim Sims is the vice president of Corporate Communications for Molycorp, Inc. Molycorp is one of the world's leading producers of custom engineered rare earth and rare metal products.

Mr. Gregory Conrad is the executive director for the Interstate Mining Commission. Senator Murkowski thought it was important to have Mr. Conrad and we're glad to have him.

Professor Rod Eggert, who Senator Udall requested, is the director of the Division of Economics and Business at the Colorado School of Mines and we're very glad that Professor Eggert is here as well.

As I say to our witnesses, we will put your prepared statements into the record in their entirety and it's going to start getting hectic here in a little bit. So if you could just summarize your principal concerns, that would be very helpful and I want everyone to know that every single word in your prepared statement will be part of the record.

OK, Professor Latiff.

STATEMENT OF MAJ. GEN. (RETIRED) ROBERT H. LATIFF, PH.D, RESEARCH PROFESSOR AND DIRECTOR FOR INTELLIGENCE COMMUNITY PROGRAMS SCHOOL OF ENGINEERING, GEORGE MASON UNIVERSITY

Mr. LATIFF. Yes sir, I will try to be brief.

Good morning Chairman Wyden, Ranking Member Murkowski and distinguished members of the committee.

I'm honored to be able to testify to this committee on a subject of great importance. My name is Robert Latiff, I'm currently a private consultant, I'm a retired Air Force Major General serving 32 years active duty mostly in research and development in weapons acquisition.

As was noted I'm also an academic with appointment at George Mason University and at the University of Notre Dame. I hold a doctorate in metallurgical engineering and materials science.

Pertinent to the interests of this committee, I'm also the former chairman of the National Materials and Manufacturing Board of the National Academies. I serve as a member of the Minerals, Metals, and Materials Society, a major professional society of materials, engineers, and scientists.

At a Strategic Materials Advisory Group, a group of former defense and government officials concerned about critical minerals and metals.

I'm here to speak in strong support of S. 1600. For several years I followed the attempts in both the House and the Senate to pass legislation on this important topic. It remains critical to national security in my opinion that this bipartisan piece of legislation be acted—enacted into law.

While the rare earth crisis of the last few years appears to have somewhat abated, we should not become complacent. The fundamental risks that result from not having a secure supply of critical materials has not gone away.

S. 1600 would require the U.S. Government to define criticality as it relates to materials, identify those materials that deems critical, and establish policies to ensure their availability. It would authorize funding for research and development and would advance work force development in areas important to materials.

In all of these actions I believe we'll have positive effects on national security and national defense. To the first point I note that the European Union published a report in 2010 that identified 14 materials and now I understand 20 that they deemed critical and recommended policies to the member Nations for their supply conservation and potential substitution. The U.S. has no such policy, nor do we have a single definition. S. 1600 is an important step in correcting that issue and establishing a coherent policy.

I've been following these issues since 2007 when I chaired a committee concerned with the national defense stockpile of the Defense Logistics Agency. Our committee was very concerned over what we felt to be DOD's continued inaction on the topic

Subsequently in a report to Congress, DOD reported that there had in fact been cases in which materials issues had impacted weapons acquisition programs in some way. However, even in the face of these materials impacts and by the then well known issues surrounding rare earth materials, DOD policy continued to be silent on the topic and insisted that market forces would be sufficient to satisfy DOD needs.

It has only been in the last year that DOD has finally agreed that the market might not be sufficiently robust to supply needs for several materials. That recognition was a positive result. However, while they may choose to stockpile materials like yttrium and dysprosium, there is still not a domestic supply of some key rare earth metals or oxides, thus it becomes essentially affixed to the supply chain.

What is needed is not just a near term fix, but also a long term solution and my hope is that S. 1600 might better inform DOD policy which could in turn lead to better availability and availability of key weapon systems.

On the subject of materials research a highlighted June 2013 report by the U.S. Air Force Chief Scientist entitled, "Global Horizons". In that report the Chief Scientist lists materials science as the first of 5 enabling technologies important to the Air Force from FY13 to FY27. The subsequent chart lists declining domestic availability of raw materials as an important key trend.

Policy makers should take note of this, clearly the services in executing their Title 10 training equip responsibilities recognizing -recognized the criticality of these issues as they are forced to deal with availability and material scarcity.

The National Materials Advisory Board and paneled a committee in 2005 on the globalization of materials research and development, which it is important to note was funded by the Department of Defense. The report of that committee quite accurately predicted an increase in the importance of materials research in other countries, along with a decreased dominance by the United States in the materials research field.

More recently a 2011 report by Thompson Reuters verified this result and concluded that while materials research publications have been on the rise worldwide, the U.S. has in fact been in decline.

I would point out to many that past DOD weapon systems from satellites to submarines, from missiles to manned aircraft have pushed the state-of-the-art in material science and the DOD historically has been a funding source and a beneficiary. The Chairman: General I apologize I just think we're going to have to have you wrap up so we can move on.

Mr. LATIFF. I am happy to wrap up and take your questions Senator.

[The prepared statement of Mr. Latiff follows:]

PREPARED STATEMENT OF MAJ. GEN. (RET) ROBERT H. LATIFF, PH.D., RESEARCH PROFESOR AND DIRECTOR FOR INTELLIGENCE COMMUNITY PROGRAMS SCHOOL OF ENGINEERING, GEORGE MASON UNIVERSITY

Good morning Chairman Wyden, Ranking Member Murkowski and distinguished members of the Committee. I am honored to be able to testify to this Committee on a subject of great importance and about which I have written and spoken frequently.

My name is Robert H. Latiff. I am currently a private consultant, providing technology and management advice to FFRDCs, universities, and private industry. I am a retired Air Force Major General, having served 32 years of active duty, largely in research and development and weapons system acquisition. I am also an academic, with appointments at George Mason University, where I teach systems acquisition and intelligence technologies, and at the University of Notre Dame where I am an adjunct professor in the Department of Philosophy. I hold a doctorate in metallurgical engineering and materials science.

Pertinent to the interests of this Committee, I am the former Chairman of the National Materials and Manufacturing Board and am a member of the Air Force Studies Board of the National Academies. I am also a member of The Minerals, Metals, and Materials Society (TMS), a major professional society of metals, minerals, and materials engineers and scientists, and of the Strategic Materials Advisory Council, a group of former senior U.S. government defense and materials officials and industry experts concerned about critical minerals and metals.

I am here to speak in strong support of S1600. For several years I have followed the attempts in both the House and Senate to pass legislation on this exceptionally important topic. For reasons I will discuss, it remains critical to national security, in my opinion, that this bi-partisan bill be enacted into law. While the rare earth crisis of the last few years appears to have somewhat abated, we should not become complacent. The fundamental risks that result from not having a secure supply of critical materials have not gone away.

S1600 would require the U.S. government to define criticality as it relates to materials, identify those materials it deems critical and establish policies to enhance the their domestic availability. It would authorize funding for research and development on those materials and would advance education and workforce development in areas important to materials. All of these actions will, I believe, have positive effects on national security and national defense. To the first point I note that the European Union published a report in 2010 that identified fourteen materials they deemed critical and recommended to the member nations broad policies for their development, recycling, conservation, and potential substitution. The U.S. has no such policy document. Nor do we have a single definition of what constitutes critical materials. S.1600 is an important step in correcting this issue and establishing a coherent national policy.

I have been following these issues since 2007 when, as a member of the National Materials Advisory Board, I chaired a committee concerned with Defense Logistics Agency's National Defense Stockpile. Our committee was very concerned over what we felt to be Department of Defense's continued inaction on the topic. Subsequently, in a report to Congress, DOD reported that there had, in fact, been cases in which materials issues had impacted weapons acquisition programs in some way. However, even in the face of these materials impacts and the by then well-known issues surrounding rare earth materials, DOD policy continued to be silent on the topic and insisted that market forces would be sufficient to satisfy DOD needs. It has only been in the last year that DOD has finally publicly agreed that the market might not be sufficiently robust to supply needs for several materials deemed extremely important to current weapon systems. That recognition was a positive result. However, while they may now choose to stockpile materials like Yttrium and Dysprosium, there still is not a domestic supply of some key rare earth metals or oxides; thus it essentially becomes a fix to the supply-chain. What is needed is not just a near-term fix, but also a long-term solution to the underlying and systemic problems. My hope would be that a national policy, such as that engendered by S1600 might better inform DOD policy, which could in turn lead to better materials security, and availability of key weapon systems. The end result of the activities required by this legislation will likely mean that the DOD would not have to depend on extraordinary measures to insure access to important materials for its weapon systems

On the subject of materials research, I highlight a June 2013 report by the USAF Chief Scientist entitled "Global Horizons". In that report, the Chief Scientist lists materials science as the first of five enabling technologies of importance to the USAF from FY13 to FY 27. A subsequent chart lists declining domestic availability of raw materials as an important key trend. Policy makers should take note of this. Clearly, the services, in executing their Title 10 "train and equip" responsibilities, recognize the criticality of these issues as they are forced to deal with availability issues and materials scarcity.

Turning again to the work of the National Academies, as early as 2005 The National Materials Advisory Board impaneled a Committee on the "Globalization of Materials Research and Development" which, it is important to note, was funded by the Department of Defense. The report of that committee quite accurately predicted an increase in importance of materials research in other countries, along with a decreasing dominance by the United States in the materials research field. More recently, a 2011 report by Thomson Reuters, verified this result and concluded that while materials research publications have been on the rise world-wide, the U.S. has in fact been in decline in regard to materials R&D. I would point out that many past DOD weapon systems, from satellites to submarines, from missiles to manned aircraft, have pushed the state of the art in materials science and that DOD historically was a significant funding source and beneficiary of advanced materials research.

On the topic of education and workforce development, I note with some dismay the decline in the number of university materials science departments in the U.S. and the steep decline in the number of materials science and engineering degrees conferred. While some of this decline can be attributed to and explained by the concomitant increase in degrees in associated fields, it remains true that knowledge of basic materials science, materials design, mining, extractive technologies, materials processing, etc. has been on the decline. While admittedly dated, a 2004 American Association for the Advancement of Science article advised graduates not to seek a job in the metals industry unless they intended to work overseas. At that time, in the previous 30 years the number of jobs for scientists working in metals had declined from more than 13,000 to fewer than 2000. This is consistent with the more recently expressed views of Dr. Karl Gschneidner of Ames Laboratory, considered to be the leading U.S. expert in rare earth materials. Policies and the requirements of S1600 to enhance education and workforce development in theses areas will have important national security as well as economic implications. A reinvigoration of materials education writ-large will also benefit DOD and its industrial base as they seek to retain or regain technical superiority in weapon systems performance.

In summary, I feel this is an extremely important piece of legislation in placing a long needed emphasis on domestic security of critical minerals. The national defense implications are, in my opinion, profound. I reiterate my support for S1600 and my hope that this bi-partisan legislation will be successful.

The CHAIRMAN. Very good.

Mr. SIMS.

STATEMENT OF JIM SIMS, VICE PRESIDENT, CORPORATE COMMUNICATIONS, MOLYCORP, INC., GREENWOOD VILLAGE, CO

Mr. SIMS. Thank you Mr. Chairman, Ranking Member Murkowski.

I'm Jim Sims I work with Molycorp, I'm glad to be here today.

S. 1600 is a solid step forward in the effort to revitalize domestic supply chains for critical materials. As many of us know the words permitting reform are often a type of third rail of politics in natural resource discussions and that's why I think this bipartisan compromise is so important and I thank the chairman, the ranking member and the other members of the committee who have put this forward. It's a good step forward if it were to be enacted.

Molycorp is a U.S. company. We recently complete construction and—of our $1.55 billion rare earth processing facility in Mountain Pass, California. We spent all private capital in building that facility, now as a result the U.S. is back in business in both mining, processing, and doing value added manufacturing of rare earth materials.

Moreover, we've worked on assembling a relatively robust vertically integrated rare supply chain that can now produce a wide range of materials from all 15 rare earths and from 5 rare metals: niobium, tantalum, rhenium, gallium, and indium. We sell these materials to U.S. and other manufacturers all around the world.

As part of our downstream supply chain we also produce a very important value added rare earth material, rare earth magnetic powders. Those are used in the construction of rare earth permanent magnets, and those magnets are increasingly vital to a wide range of technologies.

I know both of you know a lot of these technologies, but things such as direct drive wind turbines, high efficiency owned home appliances, and HVAC systems, MRI's, medical imaging devices, national defense systems, hybrids, plug in electrics, electric veal—vehicles, etc., many things, too numerous to list. The list continues to grow, by the way as new uses for these rare earth materials are found every year.

Our company walked a regulatory pathway to bring U.S. back in rare earth production for about 15 years. It took us just over 500 individual permits in order to get Mountain Pass back online, so with that back drought let me make just a couple of observations quickly.

No. 1 the fact that the U.S. is back online is important, but it's also important I think to note how the U.S. through Mountain Pass, now produces these rare earth materials. Once our facility is fully operational at full scale commercial rates and all of our chemical plants that comprise that facility are optimized, we will be able to produce rare earths with the environmental footprint that is smaller than has ever been done before and is smaller than it's done anywhere in the world.

Moreover the very technologies that we invested in, a lot of early stage capital, to shrink the environmental footprint of that production with precisely the technologies that also help to drive down our cost to production. So what we've found at Mountain Pass is that improving our environmental performance is also going to help us prove our—is also going to help us improve our competitiveness in U.S. global markets.

No. 2 there are a lot of advances being made in helping manufacturers use rare earth more efficiently and this was a big deal for our company, we've done a lot of this research ourselves. For example we're finding ways in working with downstream manufacturers on how to use less of the—of one of the more scarce rare earths called dysprosium, less of that rare earth in these permanent rare earth magnets. What that does is it allows more dysprosium to be made available for use in other magnets, and the more magnets that can be made, the more that the automotive makers and many other technologies can use these. That research is improving the efficiency of many more products, it's also helping more consumers gain the benefits that these magnets provide.

Finally let me just note there's understandably a lot of focus on the upstream side of rare earth and critical material production and that's important, and that's what this bill looks at. I would also encourage though the committee to look at the demand side or the downstream side of the critical materials equation. What I mean by that is the reality of the marketplace today is that downstream demand for these materials is what is largely driving upstream investment in their production.

Today the fact is that most rare earth materials wherever they're produced in the world are not consumed by manufacturers in the U.S., their isn't as much of a manufacturing base in the U.S. that needs these materials, it's largely overseas. So as you look at the policy implications of how to make this process better, I would encourage you to look at the downstream manufacturing demand because that helps drive supply.

Thank you very much.

[The prepared statement of Mr. Sims follows:]

PREPARED STATEMENT OF JIM SIMS, VICE PRESIDENT, CORPORATE COMMUNICATIONS, MOLYCORP, INC., GREENWOOD VILLAGE, CO

Chairman Wyden, Ranking Member Murkowski, and distinguished members of the Committee, my name is Jim Sims, and I am Vice President of Corporate Communications for Molycorp, Inc. I very much appreciate the opportunity to appear before you today to discuss S. 1600, the Critical Minerals Policy Act.

A U.S. company headquartered in Greenwood Village, Colorado, Molycorp is the only advanced material manufacturer in the world that both controls a world-class rare earth resource and can produce high-purity, custom engineered rare earth products to meet increasingly demanding and varied customer specifications. With 27 locations in 11 countries, Molycorp produces a wide variety of specialized products from 14 different rare earths (lights, mids and heavies), the transition metals yttrium and zirconium, and five rare metals (gallium, indium, rhenium, tantalum and niobium). Molycorp produces rare earth magnetic materials through its Molycorp Magnequench subsidiary, including neodymium-iron-boron (NdFeB) magnet powders used to manufacture bonded NdFeB permanent rare earth magnets. Through its joint venture with Daido Steel and the Mitsubishi Corporation, Molycorp manufactures next-generation, sintered NdFeB permanent rare earth magnets. The Company also markets and sells a line of rare earth-based water treatment products through its Molycorp Advanced Water Technologies subsidiary.

HOW S. 1600 WILL ADVANCE THE CAUSE OF DOMESTIC MINERAL SUPPLY CHAIN REVITALIZATION

Rare earth elements (REEs), and rare metals more broadly, are increasingly critical to high-tech, clean tech and advanced civilian and defense systems. While the U.S. has significantly increased its domestic production capabilities of REEs in recent years, a wide variety of critical and strategic metal and mineral supply chains are missing a domestic production component. The Critical Minerals Policy Act is a solid step forward in the effort to revitalize domestic mineral supply chains in the U.S.

Given that permitting reform is often a 'third rail' in natural resource policy discussions, the fact that a majority of both parties on this Committee have found common ground on this issue is an extraordinary achievement. It demonstrates both courage and principled leadership by the bill's authors and cosponsors. Chairman Wyden, Ranking Member Murkowski, Senators Udall and Heller, and the other original cosponsors of this bill, all deserve praise for working so hard to forge the compromise that resulted in this legislation. Your demonstration of bipartisan commitment significantly increases the chances of Congressional passage of this legislation.

On behalf of a company that walked a regulatory pathway that took 15 years and more than 500 permits to restart rare earth production in California, let me offer some observations on several elements of S. 1600:

- By launching a process to update and modernize critical minerals policies in the U.S., and by encouraging better coordination across the many federal agencies that oversee aspects of mineral development, this bill would provide additional regulatory certainty for all parties in permitting processes. Increased regulatory certainty is a must if the U.S. is to encourage greater private sector investment in domestic mineral exploration, processing, and downstream supply chains that can help meet the needs of manufacturers here in the U.S. and around the world.
- The bill recognizes that much can be done to make permitting processes more efficient, even without wholesale changes in underlying law. Requiring performance metrics for the processing of permit applications should spark new thinking and innovative ideas for reasonable reforms.
- The bill's directive to complete a comprehensive national resource assessment for each element designated as critical should help to prioritize resource opportunities for both government officials and private sector interests.
- Its focus on encouraging more efficient production and use of critical materials, development of alternative materials, and increased recycling is equally important. For a number of critical materials, increased production will need to be supplemented by these strategies to meet future global demand.
- Strengthening the education and workforce training infrastructure related to critical material, a goal of this bill, also is a high priority. The U.S. lags behind many nations in this area, which in turn can negatively impact investment decisions by private sector companies in critical material supply chain development.

THE RE-BIRTH OF U.S. RARE EARTH PRODUCTION

REEs offer a window into many of the issues listed above as well as the challenges of bringing more critical minerals and metals through permitting and into production.

The U.S. was once the world's largest producer of REEs, thanks to the rare earth production done for more than 45 years at Mountain Pass, California, home to one of the largest, richest and most readily processable REE ore bodies in the world.

Production at the original processing facility at Mountain Pass was halted in the late 1990s, and active mining of rare earth ore was suspended in 2002.

However, fast forward to today: the U.S. is back online in REE production. Construction is complete at Molycorp's new, $1.55 billion state-of-the-art rare earth processing facility at Mountain Pass, and production is ramping up. Not only that, but once this facility is up to full-scale operation and its chemical processes are fully optimized, we will be able to produce REE materials with a dramatically smaller environmental footprint and at a cost of production that will make the U.S. competitive with any REE material producer in the world.

Taking REEs from the ground, separating them from one another, and converting them to usable REE materials involves a highly complex, multi-stage series of chemical processes. The Mountain Pass facility is actually a collection of 12 operating systems that must work together both in series and in parallel. As our current rare earth production ramp-up continues, we are working to optimize and strengthen the system, improve rare earth recovery rates, improve on-time reliability, add redundancy, and increase product throughout.

In order to better understand the process by which REE ore is converted into useful REE products, a short 4.5-minute Technology Tour video outlining this process can be seen here: http://www.brainshark.com/molycorp/vu?pi=zHCzU9yV6zCQamz0.

You can also click on the photo* at left to see the Technology Tour.

All key production components of the Mountain Pass facility are operational, and we are in the process of conducting an orderly ramp-up of the many systems that work together to convert REE ore into usable products. The new facility was designed to produce at an annual rate of about 20,000 metric tons (mt) of rare earth oxide (REO) equivalent1 products. Output can vary during the ramp-up and optimization phase, and that is normal for new chemical plant start-ups. To date, the system has demonstrated an annualized production rate of 15,000 mt of REO equivalent[1] product, but we haven't sustained that rate due to the demands of process optimization. After we complete these procedures, which we expect to do in the first half of 2014, we anticipate increasing production volumes as demand requires.

TECHNOLOGY INNOVATION: REDUCED ENVIRONMENTAL FOOTPRINT

Mountain Pass may be a re-started rare earth mine, but it is by no means the same facility it was in the late 1990s. After rare earth production was halted at Mountain Pass, Molycorp scientists went back to the drawing board to design new processes and technologies that could help to dramatically shrink the environmental footprint of rare earth production.

These new technologies and process innovations, some of which have never before been used in the rare earth industry, have been successfully integrated in our new facility. They include:

- High-efficiency, on-site power generation through a clean-burning natural gas-fired Combined Heat and Power (CHP) plant. Among other things, this technology is helping us reduce our greenhouse gas emission (GHG) intensity as compared to legacy operations.
- A high-efficiency water treatment and recycling plant. This plant allow us to greatly reduce our fresh water usage and helps to recycle process water.
- An onsite chlor-alkali plant, which allows us take wastewater and convert it into the chemical reagents used in rare earth processing
- Higher rare earth recovery rates from our ore, which means that the facility can produce more rare earth products using the same amount of ore as before.
- An innovative tailings disposal system, which removes most of the water from mine tailings (for recycling) and allows tailings to be formed into a paste, which sets up into a solid substance for permanent onsite disposal. This eliminates the creation of a tailings "dam."

In short, once fully operational and optimized, this facility will operate as the world's most environmentally advanced rare earth processing complex.

TECHNOLOGY INNOVATION—GLOBALLY COMPETITIVE PRODUCTION COSTS

In addition to significantly reducing environmental externalities associated with REE production, the technology innovations developed by Molycorp also will help reduce the cost of producing REE materials at Mountain Pass. Producing REEs at a cost that is competitive in global markets is vital to the viability of any REE production facility.

For example, Molycorp dedicated a significant amount of early-stage capital to install an onsite chlor-alkali plant, which when fully operational will enable Mountain Pass to convert what was once wastewater discharge—hundreds of gallons a minute of salty water—into chemical reagents needed for rare earth processing. In essence, Molycorp has built a recycling loop at Mountain Pass that continually regenerates these reagents from wastewater and recycles virtually all of our process water.

This capability will significantly reduce the overall environmental footprint of rare earth production, as well as drive down our cost of production. By making our own reagents from wastewater, we will be able to do the following:

- Buy less reagents from the open market. (Chemical reagents are a significant portion of rare earth production costs);
- Sell excess reagents we produce; and
- Virtually eliminate wastewater disposal costs.

Additionally, this capability allows Molycorp to produce REE materials that are recognized in downstream markets for the environmentally superior manner in

---

*All photos have been retained in committee files.

[1] "Rare earth oxide equivalent" is the industry's standardized unit of measurement across all rare earth containing products. It is comparable to the oil and gas industry's "unit of measurement.

which they are produced. We believe that what is good for the environment can also be good for business.

HOW REES ARE ENABLING TECHNOLOGIES THAT INCREASE ENERGY EFFICIENCY AND LOWER POWER-RELATED EMISSIONS

One of the more exciting rare earth materials that we make from Mountain Pass ore is permanent rare earth magnetic materials, which when made into magnets can significantly improve the energy efficiency of motors, generators, compressors, and other devices. Because they also are significantly smaller than competing, less efficient "ferrite" magnet technologies, rare earth permanent magnets allow for smaller motors. This allows manufacturers to save on the use of other materials such as copper, steel, etc.

One example of the growing use of rare earth permanent magnets is in residential water circulation pumps.

In Europe, regulations now require the use of high efficiency water circulation pumps to distribute heat in buildings. The European Commission (EC) estimates that there are more than 100 million of these devices currently installed in the EU, and that their energy draw can make up between 5 and 10 percent of the typical electricity bill in households. That adds up: across the EU, these devices consume more than 50 terrawatt-hours per year of electricity, which is equivalent to about two percent of the overall electricity consumption in the EU. This amount of electricity generation equates to more than 30 million tons per year of CO_2, according to the EC.

Manufacturers are now turning to pumps that utilize rare earth permanent magnets in order to increase efficiencies. These next-generation, variable speed pumps can reduce annual electricity use by 60 percent or more, according to the EC. This equates to more than 30 TWh/year of avoided energy consumption.

Another example of rare earth materials used to increase energy efficiency is in electric motors used in automobiles. There can be dozens of individual electric motors in a modern automobile. When these motors utilize permanent rare earth magnets, instead of larger, heavier and less powerful iron-based permanent magnets, manufacturers are able to significant reduce vehicle weight. That translates into higher fuel efficiency and an enhanced ability to meet increasing stringent Corporate Average Fuel Economy (CAFé) standards. Additionally, rare earth permanent magnets allow motors to be smaller and more compact, which in turn allows more space in the passenger compartment. Hybrid electric, plug-in hybrid, and all-elective vehicles especially benefit from rare earth permanent magnets.

From a macroeconomic perspective, motors and motor-driven systems are estimated to be the single largest end use of electricity in the U.S., consuming over twice as much electricity as lighting, the second largest end use. Even small increases in the efficiency of these systems can translate into very significant reductions in energy demand and associated emissions, such as GHGs.

Energy efficiency experts and motor industry leaders agree that enhancing motor and motor-driven system efficiencies is one of the most promising—and currently overlooked—pathways to lower energy use and emissions reductions. Rare earth permanent magnets can play a key role in those efforts.

ADVANCES IN REE MATERIAL SCIENCE ARE INCREASING THE EFFICIENT USE OF SCARCE HEAVY REES

One of the most important technology advances being made today in rare earth material science relates to the use of relatively scarce heavy rare earths, such as Dysprosium, in permanent rare earth magnets. This heavy rare earth (HREE) generally exists in very small quantities relative to other rare earths in virtually all REE ore bodies. It is added in small amounts to high-performance rare earth permanent magnets that must operate in relatively higher temperature, 'under the hood' operating environments, generally those above 150°C. When added at levels between 2 percent and 10 percent, Dysprosium helps these magnets retain their magnetic power.

Given that this HREE is a truly 'rare' rare earth, and is overwhelmingly produced today in one nation (China), manufacturers have been reluctant in recent years to utilize these high-performance magnets in some applications.

Fortunately, continuing advances in REE material science, some of which are being pioneered by Molycorp scientists, are allowing magnet manufacturers to make rare earth permanent magnets with less and less Dysprosium.

Manufacturers are also finding ways to incorporate low-Dysprosium NdFeB magnets into their systems. Together, these efforts are allowing greater use of sintered NdFeB magnets with only 2 percent—4 percent Dysprosium, instead of traditional levels of 8 percent—10 percent Dysprosium. Such reductions are already having an impact on global demand levels for these scarce rare earths. With more Dysprosium available to markets, a greater number of sintered NdFeB magnets can be made and utilized in energy efficiency applications.

Also, advances in material science and engineering are expanding the use of bonded NdFeB magnets, made by Molycorp's Magnequench subsidiary, that have no Dysprosium content.

Some of the motors in a modern automobile that can utilize permanent rare earth magnets with little to no Dysprosium.

A separate technology trend is the continuing migration from tri-phosphor fluorescent lighting to LED lighting. Tri-phosphor lighting utilizes several relatively scarce rare earths, such as Terbium, Europium, and Yttrium. This continuing shift to LED lighting is already helping to soften demand, and increase the availability, of HREEs like Terbium and Yttrium.

CHALLENGES TO EXPANDING DOMESTIC REE PROCESSING CAPACITY IN THE U.S.

The most significant barrier to entry for new rare earth producers is undoubtedly the capacity to take mixed rare earth minerals out of the ground and chemically process them into separated, usable rare earth products. Virtually no two rare earth deposits are the same, and the often complex mineralogy of some deposits makes them highly challenging to chemically process. Consider these facts:

1. There are more than 200 different minerals that contain rare earths.
2. Virtually all rare earth deposits are comprised of multiple types of minerals.
3. The unique chemical structure of the rare earth-bearing minerals in an ore body can require a chemical processing facility that is unique to that deposit. Many rare earth deposits will require their own unique separate chemical processing facility.
4. Some rare earth-bearing minerals in a single deposit can require different chemical approaches to rare earth separation than other minerals found in the same deposit. Such multi-mineralogic ore bodies can be so difficult and costly to process as to be uneconomic.
5. Some rare earth-bearing minerals, including those that have a relatively higher percentage of HREEs, have never been successfully processed at the commercial scale to remove and separate the rare earths they contain.

These factors only scratch the surface of the many challenges inherent to economically extracting and separating rare earth elements from various ore bodies. From the perspective of policymakers, this underscores the importance of encouraging investment and continuing research and development in the area of rare earth chemical processing. With so many technical and economic challenges that must be met, more certainty in permitting and the overall regulatory framework would be welcomed by those seeking to bring new mines and production facilities online.

A close corollary to this is the relative lack of workforce knowledge and training in the U.S. today relative to rare earth chemical processing challenges. Fortunately, several U.S. universities, including Iowa State University, Montana State University, and the Colorado School of Mines, ably represented here today by Dr. Rod Eggert, have in recent years initiated new curricula aimed at better educating the next generation of technical leaders for work in the rare earth industry.

Additionally, the Administration‘s support for the Critical Materials Hub, housed in the Department of Energy's Ames Research Lab in Ames, Iowa and led by Dr. Alex King, also is helping to strengthen and reinforce the America's knowledge infrastructure in this area.

THE ROLE OF INCREASING GLOBALIZATION IN CRITICAL MATERIAL SUPPLY CHAINS

The increasing rare earth production at Molycorp's Mountain Pass facility, as well as new production that has come online in Malaysia by the Australian company Lynas, is helping to diversify global production of rare earths and to reduce the world's collective reliance on the world's predominant rare earth producer, China. Other nations are working to start rare earth mines and associated separations capabilities. Additionally, facilities that process rare earths into various downstream, value-added products, such rare earth metals, rare earth alloys, and rare earth magnetic materials, also have come online in various nations around the world.

One impact of such increasing globalization of vertically integrated rare earth supply chains is to provide manufacturers with multiple options for their rare earth supplies. This helps to de-risk critical material upstream supply chains and to reduce rare earth price volatility. All of these factors are helping to restore confidence in rare earth markets.

The capital market's response to the market instability of 2010 and 2011 has been to shift private capital to the development of these integrated supply chains. This has resulted in a significantly stronger global rare earth supply chain for manufacturers around the world.

SUMMARY

Thank you again, Chairman Wyden, Ranking Member Murkowski, and distinguished members of the Committee, for allowing Molycorp to present our views on S. 1600. This bipartisan legislation represents a very good step forward in the effort to revitalize domestic mineral supply chains in the U.S. It deserves bipartisan support in the Congress and should be supported by critical material producers and the manufacturing community that relies upon reliable supplies of these materials.

The CHAIRMAN. Let's do this. If I can call an audible with the indulgence of my colleagues, I have got to be in 2 other places right now. We also have the chairman of the mining subcommittee and, of course, the ranking member of the full committee here. I just wanted to ask one quick question and then we'll just continue with our witnesses.

Mr. Sims you all were the largest producer of rare earths in the country, but you shut down your operations and you've since revived it and are actively ramping up production. Why did you shut down?

Mr. SIMS. A couple of reasons Mr. Chairman, but I could probably boil them down to 2.

No. 1 Mountain Pass, that facility had some environmental issues with wastewater spills. We produce a lot of saltwater in this chemical process and there were some spills of that water and those were issues that shutdown the processing of rare earths.

Then we had a mine permit that lapsed in 2002, we didn't get that renewed in time, it was probably more our fault than anything else. So that physically stopped mining at the facility. Then when that permit was renewed in 2004 the then owners of that facility which was Unocal, Union Oil of California, looked at the global economics of rare earths and determined that they just didn't know how to make money making rare earths at that facility.

The CHAIRMAN. So the China issue had—was a factor in what you all were trying to do and that——

Mr. SIMS. A major factor Mr. Chairman.

The CHAIRMAN [continuing]. Part of the shutdown, because what we're trying to do, what Senator Murkowski and Senator Udall and I have all been a part of. Senator Manchin is trying to get more processing in the United States and it seemed to me as we looked at it that China was a big factor in that shutdown and also the price situation was a factor. Is that fair to say?

Mr. SIMS. Very fair to say and I'll say that now with the new technologies that have been developed, we're going to be able to produce rare earths at a cost that's among the lowest in the world including that in Asia and China.

The CHAIRMAN. I don't want to take time from additional witnesses, but it seems to me there are lessons here that relate to the development of other U.S. sources of rare earths and that's why our legislation is so important.

So I apologize to our other witnesses for the hectic nature of the morning. Senator Manchin is chairman of the mining subcommittee, Senator Murkowski, of course (is the key author of this legislation, and they will helm the remainder of the panel and I appreciate all the witnesses. We'll be working very closely with you.

Senator Murkowski noted an enormous amount of work has gone into this bill, literally years and we're going to get the administration, Senator Murkowski on this as well——

Senator MURKOWSKI. Yes.

The CHAIRMAN [continuing]. I appreciate your bringing up.

Senator Manchin gavel is yours and know we are in good stead with you and Senator Murkowski, thank you.

Senator MANCHIN. [Presiding]. She'll lead me straight I know that.

So what we'll do Mr. Isaacs if you would proceed now with your statement.

STATEMENT OF DAVID ISAACS, VICE PRESIDENT OF GOVERNMENT AFFAIRS, SEMICONDUCTOR INDUSTRY ASSOCIATION

Mr. ISAACS. Thank you Senator Manchin and Senator Murkowski.

My name is David Isaacs, I'm with—testifying on behalf of the Semiconductor Industry Association, we are the association of the U.S. based semiconductor companies involved in the design and manufacturing of semiconductors. As you probably know semiconductors are the key enabling technology that support all modern electronics and therefore advancements in semiconductor design and manufacturing has led to the innovations in IT, and telecommunications, and transportation, and medical devices, and national security systems.

So in addition to being a major employer and one of the country's leading exporters we are a key foundational technology that supports our overall economic strength. We very much appreciate the chairman and ranking member for convening this hearing and addressing this important legislation because the process of manufacturing and fabricating advanced semiconductors depends on the use of certain key materials, whether they are minerals or gases or chemicals that have certain unique chemical and physical properties.

In many instances there are no known substitutes for those materials and therefore having a secure and continuous supply of those materials is essential to our continued success and our continued ability to innovate, and central to the economy as a whole. As semiconductors get more and more advanced and feature sizes are at the nanoscale level, the use of materials with these unique properties becomes ever more critical.

Our views on this issue are very much informed by our recent experience with helium and as this committee well knows and thanks to the leadership of Senator Murkowski and others and Chairman Wyden this Congress was able to address that issue last year and get enacted into law one of the few bills that passed Congress to avoid a major shortage of helium.

Helium is not just used for party balloons and the like, but is critical to a number of industrial applications including semiconductors and we were facing major shortages, major price increases of that essential gas and again there—for many of our processes there were no known substitutes and so it was a really dire situation.

But again thanks to the leadership of this committee we were able to get enacted into law the helium stewardship act which avoided a very dire situation. But this was a near miss and so our interest in this bill is very much consistent with the intent of the legislation, which is to identify critical materials and develop a policy framework for avoiding future disruptions in the supply chain.

So we are taking action as an industry and working with a industry consortium known as SEMATECH and through our global technology roadmap to identify critical materials and we very much look forward to engaging in the effort that will take place under this bill to identify key materials for the semiconductor industry and develop the appropriate policies.

We very much appreciate this bill and support it and are—one point we would like to raise for your consideration as you continue with work on this bill is to ensure that the definition of critical mineral is broad enough to encompass the full range of materials that are critical to semiconductors manufacturing and other industrial applications. We very much agree with the holistic approach that the bill takes that looks not only at the extraction step but also processing and other downstream steps that could serve as bottlenecks in the supply chain.

So we very much appreciate the opportunity to testify and we're happy to answer any questions.

Thank you.

[The prepared statement of Mr. Isaacs follows:]

PREPARED STATEMENT OF DAVID ISAACS, VICE PRESIDENT OF GOVERNMENT AFFAIRS, SEMICONDUCTOR INDUSTRY ASSOCIATION

The Semiconductor Industry Association (SIA), the voice of the U.S. semiconductor industry,[1] appreciates the opportunity to testify in support of the Critical Minerals Policy Act (S.1600). We commend Ranking Member Murkowski and Chairman Wyden, as well as the large group of bipartisan co-sponsors, for introducing this important legislation and for convening this hearing. We look forward to continuing to work with this Committee to ensure that the U.S. has a secure supply of the materials that are critical to the manufacture of semiconductors and by extension the health of the U.S. semiconductor industry and the U.S. economy as a whole.

Semiconductors are the micro-circuits (sometimes referred to as "chips" or "computer chips") that are the enabling technology for all modern electronics found in computers and cell phones, transportation and health care devices, information and communications systems, and numerous aspects of our national defense. Because semiconductors are a foundational technology for virtually all areas of our economy, continued U.S. leadership in semiconductor technology is essential to America's continued global economic leadership and our national security. Semiconductors are one of the nation's top exports[2] and the industry directly employs about 250,000 employees and supports approximately 1 million indirect jobs.[3]

---

[1] SIA seeks to strengthen U.S. leadership of semiconductor design and manufacturing by working with Congress, the Administration and other key stakeholders. SIA works to encourage policies and regulations that fuel innovation, propel business and drive international competition in order to maintain a thriving semiconductor industry in the United States. Additional information on SIA is available at www.semiconductors.org.

[2] During the period 2008-12, semiconductors were the second largest export from the U.S., after aircraft. Source: U.S. International Trade Commission. Industry Defined By: NAIC Codes 336411 (Aircraft); 334413 (Semiconductors); 336111 (Automobiles); 324110 (Petroleum Refinery Products), Based from total exports revenue.

[3] http://www.semiconductors.org/clientuploads/Jobs %20Rollout/Jobs%20Issue%20Paper___April___2013.pdf.

I. Semiconductor Manufacturing and Critical Materials

Contrary to the popular perception that most high-tech manufacturing has been offshored to Asia, advanced semiconductor manufacturing remains strong and growing in the U.S.[4] The process of manufacturing semiconductors is incredibly complex, employing sophisticated equipment and techniques developed by the world's leading scientists and engineers[5] and the precise and controlled use of specific materials, chemicals, and gases that possess unique chemical and physical attributes. The semiconductor industry is innovating at the atomic level and each material used in our manufacturing is carefully selected to meet our technology needs and integrated together with high precision manufacturing tools to produce high performance semiconductors. As circuit features reach the nanoscale level,[6] the semiconductor industry's use of materials with unique properties becomes even more critical.

The building blocks of advanced semiconductors include a range of elements, including arsenic, cerium, cobalt, copper, fluorine, gallium, germanium, indium, phosphorus, silicon tantalum, tungsten, tin, titanium, and others. Our industry also relies on a number of specific chemicals and industrial gases in our production process. The materials utilized in the semiconductor manufacturing process are selected because they possess unique chemical and physical properties. In many instances, there are no known alternatives to these materials that satisfy our functional needs.

The semiconductor industry relies on a complex global supply chain that consists of numerous suppliers of materials, chemicals, and gases. Many of these materials are subject to multiple processing steps and pass through multiple hands prior to shipment to a semiconductor manufacturing facility (a "fab") for use in our manufacturing process. As a downstream user of these materials, SIA member companies are typically several steps removed from the extraction of the basic material, and therefore we believe it is important to adopt a holistic approach and look at the entire supply chain when assessing potential vulnerabilities in supply of these critical materials.

Because of our reliance on key materials—and the potential vulnerabilities in the supply of these materials—we believe that the Critical Minerals Policy Act is an important bill that warrants prompt consideration. We support the goal of the bill, which is to identify minerals that are critical to the American economy and may be subject to potential supply disruptions, and to develop a framework for policies to prevent potential disruptions to the supply of these minerals. Our industry has experienced shortages, price spikes, or other disruptions of key materials in the past, and we believe that it should be a national priority to take reasonable steps to improve the security of supply of critical materials. The implications of a supply disruption in the semiconductor industry reach far beyond our industry because so many sectors of our economy are dependent on the electronics that are enabled by semiconductors. Consequently, the ripple effects of a supply disruption can adversely impact major elements of the U.S. and global economy.

Our industry's recent experience with supply shortages in the supply of helium illustrates the potential adverse implications that may result in the disruption in the supply of critical materials for the semiconductor industry. Helium is an essential gas in the semiconductor manufacturing process, and because helium has unique functional attributes, there are no known alternatives to this gas for many of processes in our manufacturing processes. Last year our industry faced significant shortages in the supply of helium, as well as substantial price increases, as a result

---

[4] The majority of production (56 percent) from U.S. semiconductor firms is located in the United States, and the U.S. is home to more leading-edge process technology manufacturing facilities (i.e., 22 nanometer process technology or less) than any other country in the world. Source: IC Insights, Global Fab Database. SIA member companies continue to invest and expand in the U.S., with the construction of new and expanded state-of-the-art fabrication facilities across the country. Overall, U.S.-based semiconductor companies retain over 50 percent of global market share in a highly competitive market. Source: SIA/iSuppli/WSTS.

[5] The industry invests on average 22 percent of revenue in R&D, amounting to approximately $32 billion in 2012. Source: World Semiconductor Trade Statistics (WSTS) and IC Insights. Semiconductor companies receive a large number of patents each year and possess extensive patent portfolios. Six of top 15 US companies receiving patens in the U.S. were semiconductor companies. Source: US Patent and Trademark Office, compiled by IFI CLAIMS Patent Services (January 2013).

[6] Nanotechnology is the science, engineering, and technology conducted at the nanoscale, a range from 1 to 100 nanometers (nm). One nanometer is a billionth of a meter, or 10-9 of a meter.) See http://www.nano.gov/nanotech-101. Current leading edge chips have over a billion transistors on a single chip and features of 22 nanometers (nm), and the industry is engaged in ongoing development at the scale of 10 nm (i.e., 22 billionths of a meter, or roughly a 4,000th the width of a human hair). See "Moore's Law: The rule that really matters in tech (Oct. 15, 2012) (available at http://news.cnet.com/8301-11386—3-57526581-76/moores-law-the-rule-that-really-matters-in-tech/).

of several factors, including the pending closure of the Federal Helium Reserve. Our suppliers were shipping a reduced allocation at dramatically increased cost to semiconductor fabs, and despite efforts to conserve and recycle this gas or find alternatives in some processes, our industry was facing the risk of having insufficient quantities to operate. This created a very significant risk for our industry and the economy as a whole.

Fortunately, this Committee recognized the need to resolve this problem and Chairman Wyden and Ranking Member Murkowski led the successful efforts in enactment into law of the Helium Stewardship Act (PL 113-40). We greatly appreciate the leadership of this Committee in enacting this essential legislation in a timely manner. But this experience demonstrates the need to work proactively to develop the appropriate policies to avoid future disruptions to the supply of critical materials.

Our industry has also faced other disruptions in the supply of processed materials that are essential to semiconductor production. To cite one prominent example, in July 1993, an explosion at a Sumitomo Chemical plant in Japan shut down a factory that supplied over half of the world supply of a high purity resin used in semiconductor packages. The value of the resin was estimated to be only 0.26 of a penny per integrated circuit, but without the resin semiconductor production would come to a halt, a disruption that the U.S. government recognized would soon be felt in the computer, automobile, telecommunications equipment, and other manufacturing industries. Spot prices for one type of chip, dynamic random-access memory ("DRAM") memory chip nearly doubled, and DRAM buyers who did not have long term contracts were paying in excess of $300 million a week for several weeks after the explosion. Since 95 percent of world production of the high purity resin was located in Japan, there was a concerted effort by the U.S. industry and government to press Sumitomo Chemical and other Japanese suppliers to allocate remaining inventory and production transparently and fairly. In part due to long supply chains using sea freight, there was sufficient inventory to overcome the crisis until the Sumitomo Chemical resumed operations in November of 1993. This example illustrates the need for policies that adopt a holistic approach to assessing the supply chain of critical materials.

These are just a sampling of instances that illustrate the potential vulnerability of the supply chain.[7] In order to avoid future supply disruptions, SIA is pleased that this Committee is taking action to secure the supply of critical materials for the future.

II. Actions by the Semiconductor Industry to Secure Supply of Key Materials

In light of our recent experience with the shortage of helium, SIA looks forward to working with the Congress and the Administration to identify critical materials and develop the appropriate policies to secure the supply of key materials. Our industry is engaged in ongoing efforts to identify critical materials used in our processes and avoid harmful disruptions to the supply of these materials.

1. An industry consortium, SEMATECH,[8] has a Critical Materials Council that works to analyze risks to the critical materials supply chain and develop contingency plans for dealing with possible disruptions.
2. The industry's technology roadmap, the International Technology Roadmap for Semiconductors (ITRS),[9] includes a chapter on emerging materials that will be needed for future innovations in our industry.

SIA is leveraging these ongoing efforts, as well as studies and reports from government and other experts,[10] to evaluate the materials critical to the semiconductor manufacturing process. Our assessment will consider of a broad range of factors, including the following:

- The nature, type, and amount of usage in the semiconductor industry

[7] Another example was the result of Hurricane Katrina, which caused extensive damage to a major liquid hydrogen facility in New Orleans. Coupled with a previously planned closure of another plant in Canada, the damage to this plant caused a shortage of supplies of liquid hydrogen. More recently, the industry is concerned by actions such as the recent announcement by China to reduce the export quota for rare earth minerals. See http://www.bloomberg.com/news/2013-12-13/china-cuts-first-batch-rare-earth-export-quota-for-second-year.html.

[8] See http://www.sematech.org/.

[9] See http://www.itrs.net/.

[10] See, e.g., U.S. Department of Energy, Critical Materials Strategy (December 2011) (available at http://energy.gov/sites/prod/files/DOE_CMS2011_FINAL_Full.pdf); U.S. Geological Survey Minerals Information (available at http://minerals.usgs.gov/minerals/).

- The availability of alternatives to the material to satisfy the industry's functional requirements
- The degree of reliance on imports of the material
- The geographic concentration and location of sources of the material
- The nature of the supply chain and potential vulnerabilities in supply
- Known worldwide reserves and anticipated future supplies
- Current consumption and expected future demand
- Percentage of U.S. consumption of the material, and the usage in the semiconductor industry as compared with other uses
- Price and price trends
- Past incidents of supply disruptions or price spikes

As we continue with this process and identify critical materials and potential vulnerabilities in the supply of these materials, we hope that our recommendations will be considered for inclusion in the lists compiled by the Secretary under this bill.

III. SIA Suggestions on the Critical Minerals Policy Act

SIA offers the following suggestions for the consideration of the Committee as you continue work on S. 1600.

1. Definition of "critical mineral"

The bill defines a "critical mineral" as "any mineral or element" designated as critical, with exclusions for materials that are fuels or water. While this definition is broad, we believe that it is important to ensure that this definition is sufficiently broad to encompass the full range of materials that are critical to the semiconductor industry. The semiconductor industry relies on a range of chemicals, gases, and other materials that may fall outside the definition of a "mineral" or "element." For example, drawing on the recent experience with helium, it is possible that this gas might fall outside the definition of "mineral." Alternatively, even if it was captured by the term "element," it is possible that it may be excluded as a "fuel," since it is typically co-located with natural gas and extracted as a byproduct of the natural gas extraction process. There may be other materials or compounds that are essential to the semiconductor manufacturing process that might inadvertently fall outside the definition of this term. Accordingly, we request that the definition of "critical mineral" (or "critical material") is broad enough to capture the full range of materials that are critical to semiconductor manufacturing and the U.S. economy as a whole.

2. Definition of "critical mineral manufacturing"

Section 101(a)(2) defines "critical mineral manufacturing" specifically cites a number of important sectors of the economy, including "consumer electronics." Semiconductors play a pivotal role in all the listed sectors, including consumer electronics. Nonetheless, we believe that this term should be broadened to encompass the full range of electronics that are critical to our economy, not only consumer electronics. For example, the bill omits transportation and information technology, two important sectors that are reliant on innovations enabled by semiconductors. Some of these sectors may not be consumer focused but still have semiconductors as an essential component.

We further note that Section 101(a)(2), regarding the draft methodology for designating critical minerals, employs the same reference to "consumer electronics" regarding "important uses" of these minerals. This list should also be expanded to include a broader range of sectors that rely on semiconductors, information technology, and electronics.

3. Criteria for Designation as "Critical"

Section 101(a) sets forth the factors to be considered in the methodology for designation as "critical," with a focus on minerals that may be subject to supply restrictions and are used in important economic sectors. SIA agrees with this general approach, and suggests that these criteria should be made more detailed to encompass a broader range of factors that could warrant a designation as a critical mineral. Pages 3-4 of our testimony lists a number of factors that we believe should be considered. We also urge the Committee to take a holistic approach to evaluating the supply chain that supplies critical materials to the semiconductor industry and other sectors, because vulnerabilities in the supply may occur far beyond the extraction of the material.

4. Policy Changes to Address Critical Minerals

Section 102 enumerates certain policy changes in response to the designation of a mineral as critical, such as changes to the National Materials and Minerals Policy,

Research and Development Act of 1980. Similarly, Section 106 calls for a study by the National Academies of Science to update its report on "Hardrock Mining on Federal Lands." We agree that these measures may be appropriate, but the bill should address the full range of policies that could impact critical materials, whether or not they pertain to minerals and minerals extraction. Once again, drawing on the helium example, we suggest that the bill should be broad enough and flexible enough to trigger appropriate revisions to policies relating to helium, such as the Helium Stewardship Act.

5. Recycling, Efficiency, and Supply

Section 106 calls for the Secretary of Energy to conduct a research and development program "to promote the efficient production, use, and recycling of critical minerals throughout the supply chain." We agree that such a study could be beneficial to improving the efficiency in the use of critical materials. Among other things, reforming the rules governing the import and export of used electronics for recycling could facilitate the recovery of valuable materials contained in these products. We should exercise caution, however, before imposing new or ill-advised mandates on the use, labeling, reuse, or recycling of these materials.

6. Alternatives

Section 107 calls for the Department of Energy to conduct a study on potential alternatives to critical minerals. We strongly support research to evaluate alternatives to certain critical materials. Because our industry selects materials because of their unique physical and chemical properties, there may not be suitable alternatives in the semiconductor industry. Nonetheless, we support additional research in this area.

We note that the study called for in Section 107 appears to be limited solely to critical minerals in energy technologies. This is certainly one essential area for study, but the bill should call for an assessment of potential alternatives in the full range of critical mineral manufacturing.

Thank you for the opportunity to offer this testimony on behalf of the U.S. semiconductor industry, and we look forward to working with the Committee as it works on this important bill.

Senator MANCHIN. Thank you Mr. Isaacs.

STATEMENT OF GREGORY CONRAD, EXECUTIVE DIRECTOR INTERSTATE MINING COMPACT COMMISSION, AND ON BEHALF OF ALASKA DEPARTMENT OF NATURAL RESOURCES, ANCHORAGE, AK

Mr. CONRAD. Good morning Mr. Chairman, Ranking Member Murkowski.

My name is Gregory Conrad and I serve as executive director of the Interstate Mining Compact Commission which is a multiple—multi-governmental organization representing the natural resource and environmental protection interest of our 26 member States.

I'm pinch hitting today for Robert Swenson, the Deputy Commissioner of the Alaska Department of Natural Resources who was supposed to appear before you but due to weather in Juneau had several flights canceled and was unable to be here and he sends his apologies.

On behalf of Governor Sean Parnell the State of Alaska and the 26 member States of the IMCC we appreciate this opportunity to testify in strong support of S. 1600. As State governments we have a significant stake in this debate and we applaud this bipartisan effort to revitalize the United States critical minerals supply chain and reduce the Nation's dependence on foreign supply. In the face of growing resource nationalism abroad, it is crucial that the United States take steps to account for, protect and further bolster domestic sources of critical minerals.

Developing our Nation's mineral wealth in a manner that maximizes access to minerals while maintaining environmental responsibility must be a fundamental component of our efforts to sure up national mineral resource security.

My testimony today will address why this legislation is necessary and timely. In particular I will outline complimentary efforts the State of Alaska is undertaking through its strategic minerals initiative launched by Governor Parnell in 2011.

Some of these same efforts are also being pursued in similar ways by other IMCC member States. Recognizing the Nation's need for domestic production of strategic and critical minerals and the significant minerals potential in Alaska, Governor Parnell announced a 5 part initiative to assess, incentivize, and develop strategic minerals in Alaska.

This initiative includes undertaking a statewide assessment of Alaska's strategic mineral potential, supporting the development of known and highly perspective strategic mineral occurrences through infrastructure partnerships and incentives, improving the structure and efficiency of the permitting process, deepening partnerships in cooperation with the Federal Government and other stakeholders to encourage domestic exploration, development, and processing of rare earth elements and other strategic minerals, and attracting new investment in markets for Alaska's abundant mineral resources.

Our hope is that this committee can use Alaska's strategic minerals initiative as an example of successful government investment in the mineral sector, engage the level of investment needed to address the national effort.

Our first critical component of Alaska's strategic minerals initiative was the State's strategic and critical minerals assessment project compiling existing datasets was a first key step in the process, and it allowed the State to focus limited funds on highly perspective State lands that are open to mineral exploration. Partnering with Federal agencies was also an important step to ensure that geopolitical boundaries do not hinder the geological analysis.

The State's efforts to provide publicly available high quality and consistent digital geologic datasets will allow policymakers and land managers to make informed decisions, spur minerals exploration, and subsequent mine development, and ultimately reduce the Nation's reliance on foreign supply.

Since project initiation in 2012 Alaska has spent $3.8 million on field investigations and as a result over 3.9 million acres have been assessed and more than 1.6 million acres of high resolution air borne geophysics has been required for a total of 5.5 million acres of mapping.

To contemplate similar programs for our nationwide effort significantly more funding and boots on the ground will be necessary. S. 1600 would move us in this direction in meaningful ways but enhanced funding is a must.

Turning to another significant aspect of S. 1600 Governor Parnell initiated a statewide permitting initiative in 2010 that called on State resource agencies to evaluate their permitting process to make them more timely, predictable, and efficient. Legislative support has been essential for Alaska to make these improvements, and in Fiscal Year 2012 the Alaska Legislature provided significant funding for the State to create efficiencies in the permitting process.

Since 2011 Department of Natural Resources has been able to reduce its backlog on permits and authorizations by more than 50 percent. Alaska has also worked with miners and several State and Federal agencies to modernize Alaska's mine permitting forms. This change has simplified the process for miners, eliminated or simplified duplicative and confusing technical terms, and will improve application processing by reducing areas-errors and increasing readability. We believe that S. 1600 would similarly provide relief in this manner.

As domestic needs and supply constraints evolve it is imperative the government is ready with the data and regulatory environment necessary to address the unique challenges and meet the Nations need for domestic resources. S. 1600 is a much needed bipartisan effort to address this and is an example through Alaska's efforts on how this effort might work on a national scale.

In closing I would like to submit a statement for the record reflecting the position of IMCC on this important legislation.

Thank you for the opportunity to testify today.

[The prepared statement of Mr. Swenson follows:]

PREPARED STATEMENT OF ROBERT SWENSON, DEPUTY COMMISSIONER, ALASKA DEPARTMENT OF NATURAL RESOURCES, ANCHORAGE, AK

I. Introduction

Chairman Wyden, Ranking Member Murkowski, and honorable members of the Senate Committee on Energy and Mineral Resources—My name is Robert Swenson and I am Deputy Commissioner of the Alaska Department of Natural Resources (AK DNR). On behalf of Governor Sean Parnell, thank you for this opportunity to testify in strong support of the Critical Minerals Policy Act of 2013. We applaud this bipartisan effort to revitalize the United States' critical minerals supply chain and reduce the nation's dependence on foreign supply.

I have also been entrusted by the 26 member and associate-member states of the Interstate Mining Compact Commission (IMCC) to convey their views to the Subcommittee today, and to express their gratitude for your leadership in this area, as well as their strong support for S. 1600.

Strategic and critical minerals (SCM) are those minerals determined to be essential for use in the United States but subject to potential supply disruptions. The U.S. Geological Survey (USGS) maintains a list of critical minerals that is updated on the basis of supply risk and changing technologies. The list includes rare-earth elements, the platinum-group metals, graphite, and 13 other elements or element groups. It is worth noting that these are just a subset of the 36 elements identified by the USGS for which the United States imports more than 70 percent of its supply, and that this list will change over time based on supply and the evolution of demand.

II. Overview of Today's Testimony

My testimony today will address why this legislation is necessary and timely. I will also outline very similar and complementary efforts the State of Alaska is undertaking through its strategic minerals initiative launched by Governor Parnell in 2011. My primary objective is to share specific examples of how government investment can significantly improve our understanding of resource potential, ensure protection of the environment, and encourage private sector investment to help meet our mineral commodity needs.

Before getting into substantive matters, I would like to briefly mention my professional background as it pertains to this testimony and provide some information about the IMCC.

As the State Geologist and now Deputy Commissioner of AK DNR, a state agency employing more than 1,100 resource professionals, I have been in charge of designing and implementing the State of Alaska's strategic and critical mineral effort. The AK DNR workforce includes scientists with expertise in conducting geological mapping and airborne geophysical studies as well as experts in permitting who work to ensure that exploration and development is conducted in a manner that is compatible with Alaska's unique environment and stringent regulatory standards.

The IMCC, of which the State of Alaska became a full member last year, is a multi-state organization that represents the natural resource and related environmental protection interests of its member states. Twenty-one states have ratified their membership in the IMCC through acts of their respective state legislatures, and five others participate as associate members while they pursue enactment of state legislation ratifying their membership. A primary focus of the IMCC is liaising with Congress and the federal government to promote a cooperative effort between state and federal agencies in advancing responsible mining development and environmental protection.

As the primary regulators of mineral production activity within their borders, the IMCC member states have a vital interest in the development of all minerals, particularly those of strategic and critical importance to the United States. Even where minerals are produced on federal lands, states often work in concert with our various federal agency partners to ensure that these minerals are mined in an efficient and effective manner, while also protecting the environment and balancing impacts on other resources such as the land, water and air.

III. Significance of S. 1600

In its findings, S. 1600 declares that "the United States lacks a coherent national policy to assure the availability of minerals essential to manufacturing, national economic well-being and security, agricultural production, and global economic competitiveness. We strongly agree with this finding. The bill seeks to establish a new critical minerals policy that:

- Facilitates domestic production;
- Promotes investment-quality, environmentally-sound domestic mining, processing and minerals recycling;
- Establishes a national assessment for mineral demand, supply and needs; and
- Addresses permitting inefficiencies that impact the minerals sector

Our Nation's federal agencies (e.g., the USGS, the U.S. Bureau of Land Management (BLM), and the U.S. Forest Service (USFS)), will take a lead role in implementing this new policy and, to be successful, they will need to establish strong partnerships with the states that have the resource base to support a strategic minerals sector and the regulatory systems and expertise to develop those resources.

As shown in Figure 1* in the appendix to this testimony, as of 2012, the United States relied on imports for most of its strategic and critical minerals. Figure 1 is a graph from the U.S. Geological Survey's 2013 mineral commodity summary of 63 mineral commodities important to the United States. The figure shows that our nation relies on imports for 100 percent of 17 of the 63 minerals and relies on imports for more than 50 percent of 25 additional minerals. Our reliance on imported minerals, however, is not due to an absence of resource potential.

In fact, while much additional work and investment is needed to develop domestic supplies, many U.S. regions contain significant potential for strategic and critical minerals. To help understand Alaska's potential, we have modified Figure 1 to include current, past, and potential production, and highlight the commodities that are currently on the USGS list of SCMs.

IV. Alaska's Strategic and Critical Minerals Initiative

The State of Alaska is blessed with vast mineral potential on its lands. Based on USGS estimates, if Alaska was a country, it would be in the top 10 for:

- Coal (17 percent of the world's coal; 2nd most in the world)
- Copper (6 percent of the world's copper; 3rd most in the world)
- Lead (2 percent of the world's lead; 6th most in the world)
- Gold: (3 percent of the world's gold; 7th most in the world)
- Zinc: (3 percent of the world's zinc; 8th most in the world)
- Silver (2 percent of the world's silver; 8th most in the world)

In addition, Alaska has more than 70 known occurrences of rare earth elements (REEs) and multiple occurrences of SCM s, as noted on Figure 2. We expect that continued exploration will lead to additional discoveries.

---

* All figures have been retained in committee files.

Recognizing the nation's need for domestic production of SCMs and the significant minerals potential in Alaska, Governor Parnell directed the Department of Natural Resources to hold an inaugural Alaska Strategic and Critical Minerals Summit on September 30, 2011. During the summit, the governor announced Secure Alaska's Future: Strategic Minerals, a five-part initiative to assess, incentivize and develop strategic minerals in Alaska. This initiative includes:

- Undertaking a statewide assessment of Alaska's strategic mineral potential;
- Supporting the development of known and highly-prospective strategic mineral occurrences through infrastructure partnerships and incentives;
- Improving the structure and efficiency of the permitting process
- Deepening partnership and cooperation with the federal government and other stakeholders to encourage domestic exploration, development, and processing of REEs and other strategic minerals.
- Attracting new investment and markets for Alaska's abundant mineral resources

I will now give you a brief summary of these efforts as an example of what can be done with proper leadership, cooperation, and funding. My hope is that this Committee can use Alaska's Strategic Minerals Initiative as an example of successful government investment in the minerals sector and gauge the level of investment needed to address a national effort.

Statewide Assessment

Following Governor Parnell's 2011 directive, and with funding approved by the Alaska Legislature, the Alaska Division of Geological & Geophysical Surveys (DGGS) embarked on a program to better characterize Alaska's SCM endowment. The schedule and timetable for completion of the division's Strategic and Critical Minerals Assessment project is shown in Table 1**, and Exhibit A of the appendix provides a list of products that will be made available through this project.

Compiling existing data sets was a key first step in the process and it allowed the state to focus limited funds on highly-prospective state lands that are open to mineral exploration. Partnering with federal agencies was an important step to ensure that geopolitical boundaries do not hinder the geological analysis.

High-quality, district-scale geological data is lacking for most areas of Alaska with known SCM occurrences. The most basic and useful data—geologic maps—are generally not available at a scale useful for mineral exploration (1:63,360 or 1" = 1 mile). Much of the other available public data occurs in a patchwork of coverage of varying quality, vintage, and scale. The state's efforts to provide publicly available, high quality and consistent digital geologic datasets will allow policy makers and land managers to make informed decisions; spur mineral exploration and subsequent mine development; and ultimately reduce the nation's reliance on foreign supply. S. 1600 would greatly enhance and support these types of efforts and initiatives on both state and federal lands.

The Strategic and Critical Minerals Project proposal calls for spending $2.73 million a year for five years (subject to the availability of funding). Since project initiation in 2012, DGGS has spent $3.8 million on field investigations.

Results of the Assessment Program

The Strategic and Critical Minerals Project has produced a significant amount of data since its initiation in 2011. In geologic mapping at both reconnaissance and detailed scales, over 3.9 million acres have been assessed, and more than 1.6 million acres of high resolution airborne geophysics has been acquired, for a total of 5.5 million acres of mapping. To put this into context, the Commonwealth of Virginia contains approximately 27.4 million acres within its boundaries. With the available funding over a 3 year period we have been able to cover about 20 percent of the area of Virginia. In addition to the mapping effort, the state has performed modern geochemical analysis (focused on the full suite of elements) of nearly 10,000 archived and new samples collected during the mapping effort. Much of this geochemical work has been in cooperation with the USGS, which has significantly broadened the aerial coverage and distribution of the information, as shown in Figure 3.

To contemplate similar programs for a nationwide effort, significantly more funding and 'boots on the ground' would be necessary. Certainly, there is a tremendous variability in the level of data coverage and data quality across the nation, and, as a result, performing comprehensive resource assessments will require a coordinated

** All tables and exhibits have been retained in committee files.

effort and the creation of a robust funding mechanism between states and federal agencies. S. 1600 would move us in this direction in meaningful ways.

Federal funding through Statemap and data preservation

An excellent example of cooperative funding and leveraging of state and federal dollars to acquire geologic information is the National Geologic Cooperative Mapping Program. This national program has been a cornerstone of cooperation between State Geologic Surveys and the USGS and has been supported by Alaska and IMCC over the years. Another key federal program that helps to archive samples and other forms of legacy geologic and geophysical data is the National Geological & Geophysical Data Preservation Program. A tremendous amount of valuable information was acquired at a very low cost in Alaska by sampling archived materials from both the State and USGS collections. It is imperative that these cost-effective programs are maintained and sufficiently funded to address the evolving geologic needs of the nation, including the strategic minerals assessment program. Again, the provision in S. 1600 will facilitate this type of work greatly.

V. Alaska's Efforts to Improve Permitting

Statewide Permitting Reform

Governor Parnell initiated a statewide permitting initiative in 2010 that called on state resource agencies to evaluate their permitting processes to make them more timely, predictable and efficient. This effort began in earnest in 2011.

The Department of Natural Resources has pursued permitting reform in several ways: investing in our staff, modernizing our technology, and working with the Alaska Legislature to enact statutory changes. Through our work on this over-arching permitting initiative, we are also addressing the governor's Strategic Minerals initiative, which also called on state officials to make the permitting process more structured and efficient.

Legislative support has been essential for us to make these improvements. In FY12, the Alaska Legislature provided approximately $2.7 million in operating funds and $2.5 million in capital funding for our Division of Mining, Land & Water to create efficiencies in its permitting process. In FY12 and 13, the Legislature approved funding to fill vacant positions focused on permitting.

What progress have we made? Since 2011, the Department of Natural Resources has been able to reduce its backlog of permits and authorizations by more than 50 percent. Furthermore, the Alaska Legislature has approved several bills introduced by Governor Parnell to modernize our statutes. One of those bills, enacted in 2013, authorizes state agencies to evaluate the possibility of administering the federal program for permitting dredge and fill projects in surface waters and wetlands. Under this program, the state, rather than the U.S. Army Corps of Engineers, would administer many Clean Water Act Section 404 permitting responsibilities in cooperation with the U.S. Environmental Protection Agency. While this would be a major undertaking and significant new expense for the state, assuming primacy for this federal program may make permitting projects, including mining projects, in Alaska more efficient, timely, and certain.

Specifically related to mining, our Department has worked with miners and several state and federal agencies to modernize Alaska's mining permit application forms. Three previous versions of application packets used for hardrock exploration, mechanical placer mining, and suction dredge operations were consolidated into one uniform application packet in an updateable Adobe format. These new application packets are now available online for use during the 2014 mining season. This change has simplified the process for miners, eliminated or simplified duplicative and confusing technical terms, and will improve application processing by reducing errors and increasing readability. We believe that S. 1600 would similarly provide relief in this same manner.

Large Project Coordination

Alaska employs an interagency Large Mine Permitting Team (LMPT) approach to the review of permits and authorizations for mining projects. This team-based approach, to our knowledge, is unique in the nation. It is a voluntary process, at the applicant's expense, whereby the applicant enters into an agreement with DNR's Office of Project Management and Permitting (OPMP) to provide a Large Project Coordinator (LPC), who acts as the State's primary point on contact for the project. The LPC coordinates the participation of the technical LMPT members from the different state regulatory agencies, who are also funded by the applicant via the funding agreement with OPMP. When a federal Environmental Impact Statement (EIS) is required under the National Environmental Policy Act (NEPA), OPMP typically signs on as a Cooperating Agency on behalf of all of the state agencies and coordinates their participation in the NEPA environmental review. The LPC works to minimize duplication of effort by the agency representatives and to coordinate, to the degree possible, the permitting requirements and timelines of the different state and federal agencies. The State of Alaska has long felt that a federal coordinator similar to the State's LPC could help to coordinate federal permitting.

Alaska's coordinated team approach helps to increase permitting efficiencies and to ensure that permitting requirements are not overlooked. The funding agreement with OPMP also provides a means for hiring 3rd party contractors, if the state agencies lack the in-house technical expertise for reviewing and evaluating project proposals and supporting documents. A recent addition to Alaska's approach to mine permitting has been the requirement for Health Impact Assessments (HIA) which objectively evaluate the potential impacts to human health, both negative and positive, from mine development. The HIA program is housed in the Alaska Department of Health and Social Services and is staffed by public health professionals.

Because resource development projects and environmental protection are equally important to Alaska, we have invested a lot of attention to our permitting processes and feel we have a system that is thorough, balanced and efficient. In recent years, the LMPT has participated in the EIS for the Greens Creek Tailings Expansion, the re-issuance of authorizations and financial assurances for the Kensington Gold Mine, and modifications to the Fort Knox Gold Mine's Plan of Operations and Waste Management Permit. S. 1600 seems to embrace this same type of approach for federal projects and should also facilitate the permitting of projects on federal lands.

VI. Working with Federal Agencies and Industry

One of the most cost-effective ways to gather new data in remote areas with high costs of data acquisition is through partnerships and grant programs that leverage the limited funding of all interested parties. Methods for leveraging can include data sharing, direct contribution to expand programs, cost sharing through competitive grant programs, and the cooperative use of archived samples and data sets where results are shared by all parties.

In Fall 2013, DGGS leveraged its Wrangellia airborne survey by coordinating with a mineral exploration company, allowing the company to fly an airborne survey that overlapped a portion of the survey area. DGGS has obtained the results from the company's survey, at no cost, and will incorporate it in our analyses and make it available to the public. DGGS made a similar arrangement with CIRI, an Alaska Native regional corporation, for a 100-square-mile area adjacent to the state's Farewell survey area. DGGS will remain flexible and work cooperatively with other private, industry and government partners to leverage limited funding. This is an example of the multi-stakeholder approach that S. 1600 means to utilize.

DGGS maintains close working relationships with the USGS and the U.S. Bureau of Land Management (BLM) as part of the state's SCM project. Specifically, DGGS and the USGS signed two memoranda of understanding (MOU). The first is a cooperative agreement to evaluate Alaska's Strategic & Critical Minerals potential. Work includes: 1) statistically identifying SCM-related elements with high values in statewide geochemical data in order to identify areas with high SCM potential; 2) identifying areas in Alaska with geology favorable for finding SCM-related mineral deposits, and; 3) re-analyzing historic USGS samples and obtaining modern geochemical analyses to facilitate mineral exploration for SCM.

The second MOU with the USGS is a cooperative agreement to enhance DGGS geophysical surveys. The agreement formalizes a cooperative program for the USGS and DGGS to 1) collaborate on new processing of existing and any future DGGS airborne geophysical survey data, 2) collaborate on development of new interpretative products (appropriate to both agencies), and 3) provide for the ability to share appropriate confidential geophysical data and information between the geophysical personnel of both agencies.

DGGS also has an informal cooperative agreement with the BLM to document, archive, and make publically available (on DGGS's web site) all of the historic US Bureau of Mines Strategic & Critical Minerals data and publications in Alaska.

S. 1600 appears to encourage this same type of cooperation among state and federal agencies to stimulate mineral production on both state and federal lands. We are particularly supportive of those provisions in S. 1600 that would require enhanced coordination between federal government agencies such as BLM and USFS and state government agencies that have similar responsibilities for the development of mineral resources. We believe that renewed and revitalized efforts in this regard would avoid duplicative reviews, minimize paperwork and result in timelier processing of permit applications. The bill also recognizes and gives credence to the critical role played by the states with jurisdiction over mining projects.

VII. Summary

As domestic needs and supply constraints evolve, it is imperative that government is ready with the data and regulatory environment necessary to address the unique challenges and meet the nation's needs for domestic resources. For its part, the State of Alaska has invested in the assessment of its resources for many years. Historically, the federal government has made significant investments in these critical activities as well. However, to the recent failure to prioritize the USGS minerals program have created a situation where these assessments are difficult or nearly impossible to implement at a national scale.

The Critical Minerals Policy Act of 2013 is a much needed bipartisan effort to address this situation. The bill before you speaks to unique risks concerning the supply chain of critical and strategic minerals that are important for national security, protection of the environment, and economic well-being of the nation. By addressing the data requirements for resource assessments and examining the permitting process for inefficiencies that may unnecessarily hinder responsible development, this legislation will help remove some of the barriers to environmentally sound domestic production, and provide the raw materials for new technologies that will provide a host of benefits to the nation.

As stated in the bill, the federal government cannot accomplish these tasks alone. It is critical that state and federal agencies work in close cooperation, leveraging their expertise and funding to maximize efficiency. Providing sufficient federal funding and matching grant opportunities would be a crucial part of the legislation and should be contemplated for all sections of the bill, including Section 103; Resource Assessment.

Alaska's strategic minerals initiative is a good example of how this effort might work on a national scale. While Alaska's work isn't finished yet, it has: gathered the data needed to assess the mineral potential of more than 5 million acres of highly-prospective State land; addressed inefficiencies in the regulatory framework; coordinated permitting; and increased the domestic exploration and production of a host of mineral commodities, including strategic and critical minerals. The investment history depicted in Figure 4 shows that these efforts have been successful. In Alaska, exploration expenditures—the front-end risk money that leads to the next discovery and potential development—have exceeded $100 million dollars for each of the last eight consecutive years, and exceeded $300 million per year for three of those years.

The experience in many of the IMCC member states, particularly in the West, has been similar and highlights the importance of a coordinated approach for mineral development and related environmental protection. The efforts and investment contemplated by the Critical Minerals Policy Act of 2013 will help the Nation achieve similar results.

Thank you again for the opportunity to testify before this committee.

Senator MANCHIN. Thank you sir.

Ms. THOMAS.

STATEMENT OF JENNIFER THOMAS, DIRECTOR, FEDERAL GOVERNMENT AFFAIRS, THE ALLIANCE OF AUTOMOBILE MANUFACTURERS

Ms. THOMAS. Thank you Chairman Manchin and Ranking Member Murkowski.

My name is Jennifer Thomas and I am director of Federal Government Affairs to the Alliance of Automobile manufacturers, which is the trade association that represents 12 auto makers that make roughly 3 out of every 4 new vehicles sold in the U.S. every year.

On behalf of the alliance I appreciate the opportunity to offer our views on S. 1600, the Critical Minerals Policy Act of 2013 and the need for reliable and affordable access to the minerals that are vital to automobile production.

To meet the aggressive 54.5 miles per gallon fuel economy standards by model year 2025 auto makers are fully engaged in developing more advanced technology vehicles, more efficient power trains and lighter vehicle bodies. This new generation of sophisticated and fuel efficient vehicles will be increasingly reliant on a variety of commodities, many of which appear to meet the bills definition of a critical mineral.

For example various lighter weight high strength steel alloys contain a variety of minerals including chromium, nickel, and manganese, and are utilized to reduce the vehicle's weight while maintaining the integrity of a vehicle. Platinum group metals are essential components of a vehicles catalytic converter, significant reducing carbon monoxide, hydrocarbon, and nitrogen oxide emissions.

Small quantities of rare earth elements have been used in conventional vehicles for many years, but hybrids, plug-institutions, and EV's use larger quantities of rare earth elements in their electric motors and their more complicated hybrid battery systems.

Simply put minerals are the building blocks of richly every automobile on the road today. Ensuring affordable and reliable access to them is key to the continued success of the automotive sector.

We commend Senators Murkowski, Wyden, and Udall for crafting comprehensive and bipartisan legislation that will help create a more secure and domestic supply chain for critical minerals.

According to the U.S. Geological Survey, U.S. manufacturers and diverse industries are more than 50 percent reliant on imports for than 3 dozen minerals commodities. This dependency leaves the U.S. industries susceptible to potential supply disruption in producing countries, as a result of political instabilities or a significant growth in internal demand.

The Critical Minerals Policy Act promotes policies to help ensure robust and secure supply chain of domestically produced critical minerals. The Alliance supports the requirements outlined in Title 1 to establish a list of minerals critical to the U.S. economy and create analytical and forecasting capabilities to provide accurate and timely mineral information to avoid supply shortages, mitigate price volatility, and prepare for increased demand.

Every auto maker maintains a process to manage risks throughout its vast global supplier network and the existence of impartial analysis and forecasting for critical minerals similar to what EIA produces for a variety of energy sources will help industry identify risks early and ultimately manage them.

Automakers also support the DOE research programs established in Sections 106 and 107 that would facilitate the efficient production, reuse, and recycling of critical minerals as well as programs that would identify and develop suitable alternatives and thereby reducing the demand of—for critical minerals. Given the diversity of sources impacted by the availability of minerals, DOE is the right agency to coordinate with stakeholders in developing best practices and innovative approaches for using existing minerals efficiently and for introducing viable and affordable alternatives when necessary.

We greatly appreciate the opportunity to offer our views on the Critical Minerals Policy Act and the need for a robust and stable critical minerals market. Whether it's the aluminum in automotive frames, the platinum in catalytic converters, or the lithium in electric vehicle batteries minerals are essential components in every vehicle on the road today.

This sensible bipartisan legislation will help ensure reliable, affordable domestic access to critical minerals, while promoting recycling, reuse and the development of viable alternatives to help reduce their demand.

Thank you again and I'll be happy to answer any of your questions.

[The prepared statement of Ms. Thomas follows:]

PREPARED STATEMENT OF JENNIFER THOMAS, DIRECTOR, FEDERAL GOVERNMENT AFFAIRS, THE ALLIANCE OF AUTOMOBILE MANUFACTURES

Thank you, Chairman Wyden, Ranking Member Murkowski and members of the Committee. The Alliance of Automobile Manufacturers (Alliance) is a trade association of twelve car and light truck manufacturers comprised of BMW Group, Chrysler Group LLC, Ford Motor Company, General Motors Company, Jaguar Land Rover, Mazda, Mercedes-Benz USA, Mitsubishi Motors, Porsche Cars, Toyota, Volkswagen Group and Volvo Cars. Together, Alliance members account for roughly three out of every four new vehicles sold in the U.S. each year. Auto manufacturing is a cornerstone of the U.S. economy, supporting eight million private-sector jobs, $500 billion in annual compensation, and $70 billion in personal income-tax revenues. On behalf of the Alliance, I appreciate the opportunity to offer our views on S. 1600, the Critical Minerals Policy Act of 2013, and the need for reliable and affordable access to the minerals that are vital to automobile production. We applaud the Committee for the thoughtful and bipartisan approach it has taken to address this important policy issue.

Today's automobile is among the most sophisticated technology owned by consumers. Not only is it advanced from electronics, computer and connectivity standpoints, but it must also be durable and reliable. An automobile must function consistently and well in the harshest climate conditions from freezing cold to desert heat, running on the roughest roads from urban potholes to unpaved country and off-road conditions, performing at highway speeds and in congested city streets for as much as a 150,000-mile lifetime, all while meeting thousands of regulatory requirements. Virtually every aspect of the modern automobile is now high-tech, uses advanced materials and is developed through cutting-edge processes. To keep pace with ever-growing consumer demands for sophisticated new technologies, Booz & Co. found auto industry R&D spending climbed from $7.4 billion to $102 billion in 2013. By comparison, the entire global aerospace and defense industry spent roughly $25.5 billion in the same year.[1]

To meet the aggressive 54.5 miles per gallon (mpg) fleet fuel economy standards by model year (MY) 2025, automakers are fully engaged in further refining the production of vehicles and the implementation of advanced technologies—developing more hybrids, plug-in hybrids, battery electrics, fuel cell vehicles, more efficient power trains, and lighter vehicle bodies. This new generation of sophisticated, high-tech and fuel-efficient vehicles will be increasingly reliant on a variety of commodities, many of which appear to meet the bill's definition of a critical mineral. For example, various lighter-weight, high-strength steel alloys contain a variety of minerals, including molybdenum, chromium, nickel, and manganese, and are utilized to reduce vehicle weight while still maintaining the integrity of a vehicle. Platinum group metals (PGMs) are essential components of a vehicle's catalytic converter, significantly reducing carbon monoxide (CO), hydrocarbon (HC), and nitrogen oxide (NO_X) emissions. Finally, rare earth magnets are used in the electric motors found in most hybrid and electric vehicles and in the nickel metal hydride batteries utilized in current generation hybrid electric vehicles. Some current and many future hybrid and electric vehicles are expected to utilize lithium ion batteries and while they do not contain rare earth elements (REEs), lithium ion batteries do contain minerals such as cobalt and manganese, in addition to lithium. Simply put, minerals are the building blocks of virtually every automobile on the road today. Ensuring affordable and reliable access to them is key to the continued success of the automotive sector.

Automobile manufacturing is among the most capital-intensive industries. Automakers and suppliers must make substantial investments at the front end on research, design, development, testing and certification before a vehicle enters production. New technologies carry significantly higher costs, at least initially, as they are

[1] Jaruzelski, B., Loehr, J., and Holman, R. The Global Innovation 1000: Navigating the Digital Future. Booz & Co. Issue 73. Winter 2013.

developed and refined for use on the various types of vehicles needed by American consumers. Additionally, production cycles in the auto industry are five years or longer and not all vehicles are reengineered at the same time. This need for longer lead times requires increased transparency and certainty throughout the global supply chain. Any unexpected disruptions have the potential to result in significant economic harm.

We commend Senators Wyden and Murkowski for crafting comprehensive legislation that will help create a more secure domestic supply chain for critical minerals. According to the U.S. Geological Survey, U.S. manufacturers and others are more than 50 percent reliant on imports for more than three-dozen mineral commodities, including REEs, titanium, and cobalt. This dependency leaves U.S. industries susceptible to potential supply disruptions in producing countries as a result of natural disasters, political instability or market manipulation. The Critical Minerals Policy Act promotes policies to help ensure a robust and stable supply chain of domestically produced critical minerals and, thus, provides industries reliable and affordable access to critical minerals.

The Alliance supports the requirements outlined in Title I of the Critical Minerals Policy Act to establish a list of minerals critical to the U.S. economy. Following this designation, the legislation calls for an analytical and forecasting capability to be established to identify critical mineral supply and demand to ensure "informed actions be taken to avoid supply shortages, mitigate price volatility, and prepare for demand growth and other market shifts." Every automaker maintains a process to manage risk throughout its vast global supplier network. The existence of impartial analysis and forecasting for critical minerals, similar to what the U.S. Energy Information Administration (EIA) produces for various energy sources, will help industry identify risks early and ultimately manage them.

Mineral-dependent industries must manage and mitigate risks of shortages or price spikes through a variety of means, including diversifying suppliers to the maximum extent possible, using minerals efficiently throughout the production process and establishing aggressive recycling programs to recapture supplies when vehicles are taken off the road. Automakers support the Department of Energy (DOE) R&D programs established in Sections 106 and 107 of Title I that would facilitate the efficient production, use, and recycling of critical minerals and identify and develop alternative materials that can be used to reduce the demand for critical minerals. Given the diversity of sectors potentially impacted by the availability of certain minerals, DOE is the right agency to coordinate with stakeholders in developing best practices and innovative approaches for using existing critical minerals efficiently and for introducing viable and affordable alternatives when necessary.

We appreciate the opportunity to offer our views on the Critical Minerals Policy Act and the need for a robust and stable critical minerals market. Whether it's the aluminum in automotive frames, the platinum in catalytic converters, or the lithium and nickel in electric vehicle batteries, minerals are vital components in every automobile on the road today. This sensible, bipartisan legislation will help to ensure reliable and affordable domestic access to critical minerals, promote recycling, and identify and develop viable alternatives to reduce the demand for critical minerals. The Alliance stands ready to work with the Committee on this important energy and natural resources policy. Thank you again and I will be happy to answer any of your questions.

Senator MANCHIN. Thank you.

STATEMENT OF RODERICK G. EGGERT, PROFESSOR OF ECONOMICS AND BUSINESS, COLORADO SCHOOL OF MINES, AND DEPUTY DIRECTOR, CRITICAL MATERIALS INSTITUTE, AN ENERGY INNOVATION HUB OF THE DEPARTMENT OF ENERGY

Mr. EGGERT. Thank you Ms.—thank you Mr. Chairman and Ranking Member Murkowski.

My name is Rod Eggert I'm a professor of Economics and Business at Colorado School of Mines. I also am deputy director of the Critical Materials Institute, the DOE Energy Innovation Hub that Mr. Danielson discussed in Panel 1. I also chair the National Research Council Committee that prepared the 2008 study, "Minerals, Critical Minerals and the U.S. Economy".

Let me begin with my summary thoughts and then provide an explanation, my summary thoughts. S. 1600 aligns well with the recommendations of the 2008 National Research Council Study on critical materials. Also the recommendations on the 2011 expert review panel report on energy critical elements prepared by a panel of the American Physical Society and the Materials Research Society.

S. 1600 also aligns well with my previous testimony and published statements on policy in this area. Especially noteworthy I think are its wholistic and comprehensive nature and its focus on the entire supply chain.

Now for my explanation, as an economist I believe in the power and effectiveness of markets and so my inclination is to favor market solutions rather than government interventions. But markets are not panaceas, governments have the responsibility to facilitate market activities, especially in situations when markets are not or do not work well.

In the case of critical minerals and materials there are 4 areas in which I think government activities can play an important even essential role: first in the area of international trade, policy and government activities should promote undistorted trade when trade distortions distort markets. This is an important issue in a number of mineral markets, but as I realize this is outside the scope or the purview of this committee's activities, I won't say anything further on this issue.

Second, policy and government activities should strive for more efficient processes for the regulatory review of potential new mineral development activities. Foreign sources are not necessarily more risky than domestic sources but when they are, domestic sources of mineral resources can help offset risky foreign sources. Sections 104 & 105 of the proposed legislation would be an important step in this regard.

Third, policies and government activities are essential in facilitating collection and dissemination in analysis of information. There's a long tradition of government providing basic information on which sound private and public decisions are made and Sections 101, 103, and 108 address information and analysis.

Fourth and finally policy and government activities should facilitate research and education. Research and education are traditional public goods, that is investments that the private sector acting alone is likely to undersupply because the benefits of these investments are diffuse, difficult to capture, often easy to copy, risky, and far in the future. Over the longer term R&D is perhaps the key to eliminating the supply risks associated with critical minerals and materials.

Sections 106 and 107 would help focus R&D attention on a critical minerals and materials. Section 109 would help reinvigorate—Section 109 which focuses on education and work force would help reinvent—reinvigorate our intellectual on academic infrastructure in mineral resources and materials which has to some degree withered in the recent past.

So overall and to repeat my evaluation I support S. 1600, it aligns well with a number of recent expert review studies on this issue as well as my own previous published statements on critical minerals and materials.

Thank you for the opportunity to testify today, I'd be happy to answer any questions.

[The prepared statement of Mr. Eggert follows:]

PREPARED STATEMENT OF RODERICK G. EGGERT, PROFESSOR OF ECONOMICS AND BUSINESS, COLORADO SCHOOL OF MINES, AND DEPUTY DIRECTOR, CRITICAL MATERIALS INSTITUTE, AN ENERGY INNOVATION HUB OF THE DEPARTMENT OF ENERGY

Good morning, Mr. Chairman, members of the Committee, ladies and gentlemen. My name is Rod Eggert. I am a professor of economics and business at Colorado School of Mines, as well as deputy director of the Critical Materials Institute, an energy innovation hub of the U.S. Department of Energy. My area of expertise is the economics of mineral resources. In addition to my current activities related to critical minerals and materials, several years ago I participated in two review panels relevant for today's hearing. I chaired the committee of the U.S. National Research Council that prepared the 2008 report Minerals, Critical Minerals, and the U.S. Economy. I served as a member of the committee of the American Physical Society and the Materials Research Society that prepared the 2011 report Energy Critical Elements: Securing Materials for Emerging Technologies. I also testified previously on critical minerals and materials before a Subcommittee of this Committee (2010), a House Committee (2011), and a committee of the European Parliament (2011).

I organize my remarks into three sections. First, I describe the context for current concerns about critical minerals. Second, I present my views on appropriate roles for government in light of these concerns, which reflect my previous testimony and published papers. Third, I comment on S. 1600 itself.

Context

Mineral-based materials and products are becoming increasingly complex. Early cell phones in the 1980s consisted of materials that used approximately 30 elements from the periodic table; today's smart phones contain 60-70 mineral-derived elements. General Electric uses more than 70 of the first 83 elements of the periodic table in its products or processes used to make these products. In contrast, as recently as three decades ago, a typical household owned products containing perhaps only 30 or so of these elements.

New technologies and engineered materials create the potential for rapid increases in demand for some elements used previously and even now in small quantities. The most prominent-although by no means only-examples are neodymium and dysprosium in permanent magnets for electronics and high-efficiency motors; europium, terbium and yttrium in advanced lighting systems; lithium in batteries; and gallium, indium, and tellurium in thin-film photovoltaic materials.

These technological developments raise two concerns. The first is that supply will not keep up with demand growth due to the time lags involved in bringing new production capacity online or more fundamentally the basic geologic scarcity of certain elements. The second concern is that supply is insecure or risky because of fragile supply chains. The causes of fragility are several and vary from case to case: industry concentration; reliance on imports from politically risky countries, some of which impose export restrictions on primary raw materials; and reliance on by-product production. In both cases, mineral availability-or more precisely, unavailability-is a potential constraint on the development and deployment of emerging and important technologies, especially in the energy, electronics, transportation and defense sectors.

Roles for Government[1]

As an economist, I believe in the power and effectiveness of markets. Markets provide strong incentives for private investments that re-invigorate supply and reduce

[1] See Eggert (2010) and Eggert (2011), as well as two expert-panel reports in which I participated (APS/MRS 2011, NRC 2008). My testimony today overlaps considerably with views I expressed in previous testimony before (a) the Subcommittee on Energy, Committee on Energy and Natural Resources, September 30, 2010, (b) the Committee on Industry, Research, and Energy of the European Parliament, January 26, 2011, and (c) the Subcommittee on Energy and Mineral Resources, Committee on Natural Resources, U.S. House of Representatives, May 24, 2011.

supply risks. Markets encourage users of critical materials to obtain "insurance": for example, in the short term, users can maintain stockpiles, diversify sources of supply, develop jointsharing arrangements with other users, or develop tighter relations with producers. Over the longer term, users can undertake research and development to develop alternative materials that use less of, or no, elements subject to significant supply risks. Scarcity and supply risk encourage investments in mineral exploration and mine development (potentially funded by users seeking secure supplies), improved manufacturing efficiency, and recycling of manufacturing wastes and end-of-life products.

But markets are not panaceas. Government plays essential roles in facilitating market activities. For mineral resources, government can play four important roles that facilitate well-functioning markets and help ensure reliability of material supplies in the short term and availability of mineral resources in the long term:

1. Encourage undistorted international trade.—The governments of raw-materialimporting nations should fight policies of exporting countries that restrict rawmaterial exports to the detriment of users of these materials. The U.S., European, and Japanese filings with the World Trade Organization against China and its restrictions on rare-earth, molybdenum, and tungsten exports are examples.

2. Improve regulatory-approval processes for domestic resource development.—Foreign sources of supply are not necessarily more risky than domestic sources. But when foreign sources are risky, domestic production can help offset the risks associated with unreliable foreign supplies. Developing a new mine in the United States appropriately requires an approval process that allows for public participation and consideration of the potential environmental and social effects of proposed mining. This process is costly and time consuming—arguably excessively so, not just for mines but for developments in all sectors of the economy. I do not suggest that mines receive preferential treatment, rather that attention be focused on developing better ways to assess and make decisions about the various commercial, environmental, and social considerations of project development.

3. Facilitate provision of information and analysis.—I support enhancing the types of data and information the federal government collects, disseminates and analyzes. Sound decision-making requires good information. Government plays an important role in ensuring that sufficient information exists. The Department of Commerce and Department of Labor collect and publish information on the state of the national economy that informs public and private decision making, as does the Energy Information Administration in the realm of energy. With respect to mineral resources and material supply chains, I recommend (a) enhanced focus on those parts of the mineral and material life cycle that are under-represented at present including reserves and subeconomic resources, by-product and co-product primary production, stocks and flows of materials available for recycling, in-use stocks, material flows, and materials embedded in internationally traded goods and (b) periodic analysis of mineral criticality over a range of minerals. At present, the markets for most critical minerals are less-than-completely transparent, in large part because the markets are small and often involve a relatively small number of producers and users, many of which find it to their competitive advantage to keep information confidential.

4. Facilitate research and education.—I recommend that the federal government develop and fund pre-commercial activities that are likely to be underfunded by the private sector acting alone because the benefits of these activities are diffuse, difficult to capture (easy to copy), risky, and far in the future. Over the longer term, science and technology are keys to responding to concerns about the adequacy and reliability of mineral resources and mineral-based materials, to improving our ability to recycle essential yet scarce elements, and to developing alternatives to these elements.

Education and research go hand in hand. Educational programs, especially those at the graduate level, educate and train the next generation of scientists and engineers, who in the future will respond to concerns about newly emerging critical minerals. Education and research in the geosciences, mining, mineral processing and extractive metallurgy, environmental science and engineering, manufacturing, and recycling can mitigate supply risks and increase material availability. Improvements in materials design-fostered by education and research in materials science and engineering-can ease the pressures imposed by those elements and materials subject to supply risks or limited availability. Government, in addition to simply funding education and research, can play an important role in facilitating collaborations among universities, government research laboratories, and industry.

These views on appropriate roles for government are not mine alone. A common conclusion of essentially all recent studies on critical minerals and materials is to urge governments to improve and expand activities related to information and analysis, education, and research (for example, APS/MRS 2011, European Commission 2010, NRC 2008).

S. 1600, The Critical Minerals Policy Act of 2013

My views above form the conceptual lens through which I consider S. 1600, the Critical Minerals Policy Act of 2013. My specific comments:

1. Overall.—S. 1600 covers three of the four areas I discuss above. The fourth area, promoting undistorted international trade in mineral resources and materials, is outside this Committee's purview.
2. Section 101 Designations.—This section is consistent with my third role for government. I support efforts to identify minerals that are most critical in the sense that they are both (a) subject to potential supply restrictions and (b) important in use. NRC (2008) recommends this sort of evaluation and periodic re-evaluation. Japan and the European Union already carry out this type of evaluation from the perspective of the Japanese and European economies (see European Commission 2010). Periodic re-evaluation is essential, as what is "critical" changes over time as materials, products, and market conditions evolve and change.
3. Section 102 Policy.—The amendments to the National Materials and Minerals Policy, Research and Development Act of 1980 are appropriate and consistent with my views on the role of government.
4. Section 103 Resource Assessment, Section 108 Analysis and Forecasting.—These sections represent actions that are important parts of information and analysis, my third role for government.
5. Section 104 Study, Section 105 Agency Review and Reports.— The actions these sections require would be an important start to improving the efficiency of the process of regulatory approval for domestic mineral development (my second area of government action).
6. Section 106 Recycling, Efficiency and Supply, Section 107 Alternatives.—These sections are consistent with my fourth role of government. They would require the Secretary of Energy to conduct programs of research and development. The Department of Energy already funds programs in the areas identified in Section 106 and 107. Passage of S. 1600 would provide greater justification for, and allow for possible expansion of, these activities.
7. Section 109 Education and Workforce.—This section is consistent with my fourth role of government in the area of critical minerals. Over the last several decades, 8 the Unites States has lost a significant amount of its intellectual infrastructure in the area of mineral resources.
8. Section 110 International Cooperation.—Although international cooperation is not part of my conceptual framework for government involvement in critical minerals, I support it. The United States is not the only nation facing supplychain risks for mineral resources and downstream materials. No nation can expect to be, nor should strive to be, self-sufficient. Japan, the European Union, and several individual European countries, in particular, have ongoing activities in this area. There is much to learn from their efforts, and we have a responsibility to work together with our allies on mutually beneficial activities that help ensure supply chains of critical raw materials

Senator MANCHIN. Thank you, and what we'll do is I'll start out with a few questions if I may and then Senator Murkowski will fill right in.

General Latiff, I know you spent over 30 years on active duty with the Air Force and spent most of it working on research and development weapons systems acquisitions. So you truly understand how critical these minerals are. In your opinion is there adequate domestic supply right now or do we have to rely on the world's supply?

Mr. LATIFF. To answer your first question Senator, I do understand how critical they are having made several large programs, which had material shortages, I do know. I also maintain a working relationship with a number of people who are still in the acquisition business.

In terms of domestic supply the answer is clearly no. Most of what we get somewhere along the line in the supply chain is touched by foreign countries.

Senator MANCHIN. If I may interrupt, for domestic supply is it we don't have the resources in our country or we can't extract the resources because of our laws, rules, regulations, things of this sort?

Mr. LATIFF. I think it's both, there are many cases in where we're dependent for the basic materials, but there are many cases where we also have supplies or reserves in this country. But to the problem you point out, we can't extract them or process them in many cases. Then in making the final products we also again then have to send them overseas.

Senator MANCHIN. Can I ask you another question then?

Mr. LATIFF. Yes sir.

Senator MANCHIN. What prohibition does the United States—what prohibition do we have against foreign countries owning U.S. critical minerals coming and buying our reserves and controlling those reserves? If we've identified that as a critical mineral for our Nation, the consumption of our Nation, and the—and wellness of our Nation and yet we have laws and rules that prohibit us from extracting it for whatever reason, and we can't find the balance between the environment and the need of our Nation.

Then we allow foreign countries to come in and control that supply if you will, is there any laws that you know of that we prohibit them from buying critical minerals deposits?

Mr. LATIFF. Senator I would defer, I do not have the knowledge of the laws.

Senator MANCHIN. Would anybody on the committee know that, Mr. Sims?

Mr. SIMS. Senator there is a process in Federal law that's governed by a government entity called The Committee on Foreign Investment in the U.S. We know it as CFIUS. I'm not an expert on CFIUS, but I do know that that committee, that process has purview when there are proposed to be significant foreign investments in U.S. assets that are considered critical of some—at some level. So there is a process and know the CFIUS committee looks at a lot of potential investments. The history shows that sometimes they let those investments happen and other times they don't.

Senator MANCHIN. The reason I know that much, Virginia we have law for some of the world's best coking coal to make steel. Most of that has been purchased by foreign countries, and I don't—I didn't know there was any interference whatsoever with that, it was just a matter of transaction, as if they were dealing with a neighbor next door.

Mr. SIMS. Yes.

Senator MANCHIN. It didn't make any sense to me whatsoever to set here and watch that happen, but—and you—Senator Wyden asked you the question I think you answered it you know why—the reasons and everything. You're probably in a better position to evaluate these minerals I mean the deposits that we have they are so critical to our economy and to the everyday use of Americans.

You find it extremely hard to get through the permitting process and the review and the EPA process.

Are they working with you or do you feel like you're fighting them continuously? Don't be afraid because I—we fight them every minute of every day.

Mr. SIMS. No I appreciate that Senator, I appreciate that. I have to say that it took us 15 years to get Mountain Pass, California back up and running in making rare earth prior to that Mountain pass——

Senator MANCHIN. What—you know what were you producing, what are you extracting?

Mr. SIMS. Rare earth elements.

Senator MANCHIN. OK.

Mr. SIMS. In virtually all deposits of rare earths all of the naturally occurring rare earths are all combined together, so you make one you've got to make most of the others——

Senator MANCHIN. Sure.

Mr. SIMS [continuing]. If not all of them. I experienced—

Senator MANCHIN. The things your products—things that your raw material is used for give me an example of some of—

Mr. SIMS. Advanced wind turbines, automobiles, the little ear buds that my kids put in so they can claim that they're not hearing me.

Senator MANCHIN. Everything that we depend for quality of life we have today.

Mr. SIMS. Absolutely, absolutely.

Senator MANCHIN. It almost took you 15 years to get through the permitting process.

Mr. SIMS. It is, but I would say Senator, it's fair to say that part of that was our fault as well.

Senator MANCHIN. Sure.

Mr. SIMS. We actually worked very cooperatively, we tried to and I think successfully with a lot of local stakeholders and we changed our permit application as we went forward in response to request by stakeholders. That helped us get to the end result. We also changed our technology and advanced it as we went forward so we had to apply for different permits. It was a give and take, it took a little longer than we would have liked, but we did get through the end of the process.

Senator MANCHIN. My time is up and I'll go for the second round, I want to turn it over to Senator Murkowski who I'm a proud cosponsor on this bill with her and I appreciate she bringing it back to our attention.

Senator.

Senator MURKOWSKI. Thank you.

It's encouraging to hear from each of you, your support for the legislation. As I mentioned in my opening comments I think we—there's been a lot of give and take and going back and forth and trying to build a bill that is reasonable, rational, and has support and gagging from the various industries and academia that you represent, it's clear that we've struck the right cord. Now we need to work a little bit with the administration here so that we can get a positive yes answer from DOE, but we'll work on that.

Mr. Isaacs I want to specifically note your comments and how the issue with the helium bill and how we were really on the edge of something bad happening if we were not to have dealt with that situation in a timely manner and how that kind of feeds into not only this debate about how we proceed with our critical minerals, but hopefully making sure that we're connecting the dots.

Again, whether we're talking about the auto industry or semiconductors the acknowledgement that these critical minerals which I think the only thing that a lot of us used to know about them was that they were difficult to pronounce and all seemed to end an um. But beyond that what are they, what do they do and I think that there's clearly a growing awareness, but we have more to do in helping people understand the significance and the importance of these critical elements, so the connect with what we did with helium I think is particularly important.

Mr. Sims relating the situation with Molycorp I think is helpful to us here on the committee, 500 permits, 15 years to kind of work everything through should tell us something, but I also appreciate you saying look that not all of this was government inaction in fairness there were other factors in play here. I am assuming that you have read our 40 page bill and I would be curious to know what your reaction is to the permitting section of the bill, do you think we hit the right note here?

Mr. SIMS. Senator Murkowski I think you did, I mean I think when Congress looks at any of these issues related to reforms or permitting processes you have to look through that—you have to look through the lens of what's politically possible as well. This bill does not seek to make any major changes in underlying law like NEPA Etcetera. But there are a lot of things that can be done without those changes being made, it would be highly controversial, but a lot of things could be done in the process itself and I think the bill points to those.

I think at the end of the day whatever the law says about permitting it really comes down as we found to whether you can build a level of trust between the permit applicant, the regulator, and other stakeholders at the table. Having said that to have as your bill does call for performance metrics of how the process is working is very important. To have—it points to—it encourages folks to look creatively—I think within the confines of current law as to how to make this process better. One thing that could be done now is for example to have the various considerations by Federal agencies of NEPA applications to be done concurrently as opposed to consecutively.

Now there are cases when that doesn't work, but most cases where it does that would make a very big difference. I'm sure most folks in my situation would say it'd make a huge difference that doesn't require any change in fundamental underlying law. So I think your bill is encouraging folks to be creative on both sides of the table as to how to make that go faster.

Senator MURKOWSKI. Let me ask you Mr. Conrad for the Alaska perspective and I appreciate you pinch hitting here for Mr. Swenson. This is the time of year that Juneau is sucked in, maybe it's because the legislature is in session but that's neither here nor there.

You hit on several initiatives that the Governor has advanced in terms of statewide assessment which I think is critically important, I'm curious to know if you think that when it comes to the data that is so important in making sure that we have collected sufficient amounts of geologic data to really form out the actions moving forward when it comes to accessing our critical minerals, also if you could speak to the permitting issue that Mr. Sims has just addressed.

When we think about the hurdles to accessing our—any or our minerals in the state of Alaska, there are hurdles that are out there but I think the most significant that I hear from people about is the permitting process. If you can speak to not only the data collection and whether or not we're doing a good job there and also from a permitting perspective if we are moving ourselves up from that dead last position that I mentioned in my opening comments in terms of getting responses on our mineral opportunities.

Mr. CONRAD. Thank you Senator.

The States have also been—often been we refer to is the laboratories of democracy, the laboratories of invention and I think Alaska is a perfect example of the State that has taken great strides to address both of those issues. To first identify the importance of the need for modern data and how we are able to access that data, which is sometimes a matter of resources and sometimes a matter of technology. Often a matter of working cooperatively with other stakeholders and particularly our Federal partners to achieve the type, and the level, and the quality of data that we need.

Alaska has made great strides in that area has identified not only the need, but how to go about finding this data, addressing this data and the innovative approaches that are necessary to make that happen.

On the permitting side, again Alaska has had great success in using a cooperative approach within its—within the State itself in developing an interagency approach to how permitting should be handled within the States to coordinate among all the agencies that are critical to the development and the permitting of a mine, especially a large scale mine.

Again I think has demonstrated that that kind of an approach at the Federal level would be very helpful in achieving the type of coordination that we need to move that process forward and more effectively. We believe that S. 1600 addresses both of those matters in significant ways. If we can couple that with some additional funding to assist with some of this work that we need to do particularly in the data area, we'll be well on our way to making, we believe—

Senator MANCHIN. Right.

Mr. CONRAD [continuing]. Some significant strides here.

Senator MURKOWSKI. Good, good, thank you.

I—we'll have another question——

Senator MANCHIN. Sure, sure.

Senator MURKOWSKI [continuing]. But I'll defer it to you.

Senator MANCHIN. Just very quickly, so you're saying that basically the Mining Compact Commission endorses the legislation as written?

Mr. CONRAD. Yes in our statement that I've supplied for the record.

Senator MANCHIN. Thank you very much.

Also, to Mr. Isaacs this—maybe you and Ms. Thomas might want to chime in on this one, but changing, you know we hear so much about changing the cooperate tax laws and it'll bring industry, and bring jobs back, and bring manufacturing back. But we're finding out now if we don't have the critical minerals here to provide we can do all we might and you can't come unless you have the resources here to do what you need to do.

Do you think it's adequate, I mean we have adequate supplies to be able to bring you back if we have balance in our corporate laws too our corporate tax laws that would give you the incentives to bring those jobs back to America?

Mr. ISAACS. Senator first of all semiconductor manufacturing is alive and well in the U.S. We are the world and either the number, No. 2, or number 3 exporter of the United States, so—and the industry continues to grow and particularly at the leading edge of advanced semiconductor manufacturing. But having said that, there's obviously a host of policies including——

Senator MANCHIN. Are you concerned about supply?

Mr. ISAACS. Yes, absolutely and we employ a global supply chain that's highly complex, and therefore, domestic supply is critical, but it's only part of the holistic approach that needs to be taken, which you know we really need to be taking a global look at this and making sure that the supply chain is secure around the world.

Senator MANCHIN. What would—where is the—where's your largest suppliers? Where do you buy most of your raw materials?

We'll just say the industry itself, what country does it depend on, next to us?

Mr. ISAACS. I'm not sure I can fully answer that question, but you know——

Senator MANCHIN. We hear——

Mr. ISAACS [continuing]. One thing to keep in mind——

Senator MANCHIN [continuing]. So much about China.

Mr. ISAACS. One thing to keep in mind is that we are typically several steps removed from the extraction of the raw material from the ground. I think the helium situation was a rare instance where we were maybe one or 2 steps removed from the extraction from the ground. But in most cases we depend on various steps of extraction, processing, refining to get the type of material that we need. So where it's originally—the original source of the material we'd have to do some more research into that.

Senator MANCHIN. If you could do that for us it would help because I'm sure you're falling and in case we have for our trade agreements or any type of relationships we have with some of these countries that we depend on heavily, it doesn't go quite right.

What position does that put our country in, our government we've seen what we've done with energy, with oil hasn't been too good when we needed it, so we hope we don't get in a situation with rare earth minerals too and we would hope you would advise us on that where your dependency is and what critical factor it would have if you couldn't get it.

Mr. ISAACS. Yes, thank you and as I mentioned before we are working with our industry technical consortion to look at the materials in our supply chain and look at the sources of those materials and we hope to feed that into this process.

Senator MANCHIN. Ms. Thomas do you want to comment on supply, what you believe it should have on your supply chain as far as the manufacturing and volume goes?

Ms. THOMAS. I would just add that we are also very concerned about supply shortages and you know we also have a very complex global network of suppliers and you know greater transparency in sharing of real time information is very valuable to—throughout the supply chain, so I think the information that would be generated through a lot of the programs and this legislation would provide you know valuable.

Senator MANCHIN. Can you give us a little bit of an inventory, maybe you can check with your suppliers basically on what—I mean on your manufacturers where their supply chain comes from. Most of the minerals are in——

Ms. THOMAS. Sure I mean——

Senator MANCHIN [continuing]. Much of the material they use.

Ms. THOMAS. Yes, that's a question more for our suppliers and I'd certainly be happy——

Senator MANCHIN [continuing]. I hope you would.

Ms. THOMAS [continuing]. To get back to you with that.

Senator MANCHIN. That would help us along as we proceed.

Dr. Eggert, I know that legislation expands academic programs related to critical minerals including the traditional academic programs and also our work force training which is so needed. How do you see the investment education impacting the development of our critical minerals? How would you see that happening?

Mr. EGGERT. I think an investment in education is essential. It takes a number of complimentary ingredients to develop a mine to create a successful mineral processing or manufacturing activity. It's not just the raw material, but it's an educated and trained work force and in many of the minerals and materials disciplines we've allowed the academic infrastructure to some degree to wither over the last several decades. So I think a trained and educated work force is an essential ingredient in mining and manufacturing.

Senator MANCHIN. An investment that pays off right?

Mr. EGGERT. Yes.

Senator MANCHIN. Thank you.

Thank all of you for your testimony.

Senator MURKOWSKI. Dr. Eggert let me continue with you I'm assuming coming from School of Mines that you have to a certain extent, tracked historical levels of mining activity throughout the country? Is that fair?

Mr. EGGERT. To some degree yes.

Senator MURKOWSKI. Can—then to the degree that you're able, can you give the committee any assessment in terms of what you have seen over a period of time, how mining activity in the industry within the country has changed and the reasons that we've seen decline or increase in certain areas, and I don't expect you to give me more than 45 seconds here, so if you can distill it, what changes we're seeing and why?

Mr. EGGERT. OK, first the level of investment in the mining industry tends to be very selectable to the United States and elsewhere and the United States in that regard has not been much different than other countries around the world. Having said that the U.S. share of total worldwide mineral investment has as a general rule been declining, part of that I think can be attributed to the more stringent environmental and other social permitting requirements necessary for mineral development.

But also to be fair over the last several decades a number of other countries have opened up their borders to mineral investment. Areas that had been underexplored in the past, a past when Canada, the United States, Australia, South Africa were the major destinations of investments. So part of the declined in the U.S. share of investment I think has to be attributed to good opportunities elsewhere.

Senator MURKOWSKI. Let me ask you Mr. Conrad from the Alaska perspective just some of the trends that we're seeing within the state in terms of the private investment that we recognize is key, you cannot make any of this happen unless you've got the investment side. What has helped to either bring new companies, new investment to this state, what has hurt investment opportunities within the mining industry?

Mr. CONRAD. Thank you Senator Murkowski.

Let me just give you an overview perspective that Bob Swenson provided to me in preparation for the hearing and where he noted that the mining investment in Alaska right now is primarily on state and private land as opposed to Federal land. If you look at some of the figures that are provided in his testimony you would note that the total area of state mining claims and prospecting sites for 2012 was about 4,500,000 acres, whereas the total area on Federal lands for 2012 was about 168 thousand acres.

That's attributable primarily from his perspective, and I think in general from Alaska's perspective to the need for governmental support in supplying the kind of modern data that we need and do not yet have, land access, and then permitting efficiencies in terms of attracting investment. When those things don't line up well, it has a negative impact on that investment activity.

Senator MURKOWSKI. One question and this will be my last, I put it out to all of you it's what I asked both on the first panel and this was the issue of forecasting and better—trying to better understand what we might need in terms of these critical minerals. Again recognizing that we're doing a lot of work to find substitutes, a lot of work to reuse, recycle, but the issue of being better able to forecast.

Again we've got different industries that are represented at the table here, but how can we do a better job of forward thinking in terms of being able to anticipate what it is that we will need so that we avoid the threat of an imminent crisis like we almost had with helium? I'll throw it out to whoever wants to start.

Mr. Isaacs, I'll pick on you.

Mr. ISAACS. We very much rely on the USGS and other expert sources of information and again we as I mentioned earlier we have an exercise called the International Technology Roadmap for Semiconductors which includes a chapter that looks at emerging materials that will be critical to the next generation of semiconductors, so that's our attempt to forecast to the future and what we'd like to do is integrate that effort with the exercise under this bill to identify the materials that are most critical for our industry and develop the appropriate policies to avoid vulnerabilities going forward.

Senator MURKOWSKI. So Mr. Sims from the producer side you know you're getting push from industry that says we need it, we need it, how do we get more folks like Molycorp engaged?

Mr. SIMS. I think it's fair to say that at least in our little world of rare earths that virtually all independent forecast show significantly increasing demand for most of those, so the signals is out to us as producers to try to produce more and to try to do more recycling which we're involved with and some other technologies. Getting the capital, the private capital necessary to bring some of these projects online is difficult.

We went through a several year process of raising about over $1.5 billion all in the private capital markets, that is not easy to do. But there are companies that are out there trying to do it right now and a lot of it depends on the value and the perceived quality of the resource. But in terms of downstream forecasting of demand anything the government can do that would help us in the private sector understand the broader perspective that would be very helpful.

Senator MURKOWSKI. General Latiff from the defense side, the security side.

Mr. LATIFF. Senator the number of DOD Weapons Systems is small enough, but it's not going to drive demand significantly for a lot of these minerals, so I'll answer a different question and that is that some of the weapons systems that we have are so critically dependent on some of these materials for their performance, and so it is important to the DOD to know what future availability of these materials is going to be as they plan their weapons systems which go out as you know for many years.

Senator MURKOWSKI. Right.

Anybody else want to weigh in?

Ms. Thomas.

Ms. THOMAS. Yes I'll just add that it would be extremely helpful to the automakers and our suppliers in providing you know information on availability and allow us to identify risks early on and ultimately manage them properly.

Senator MURKOWSKI. OK, good.

Dr. Eggert you can wrap it up.

Mr. EGGERT. A supplementary point, I think many of the markets for the minerals and materials that we're talking about are not very transparent. The supply chain risks are often hiding because the final purchaser is 5 or 6 steps removed from the initial mining and to some degree, and I don't want to overstate the point, but to some degree it's like what happened with—during the financial crises the risks were buried and not obvious to all involved and through forecasting and scenario building one can help make these supply chains more transparent and allow all participants to better manage their risks.

Senator MURKOWSKI. That's an excellent point. It's a good way to end this conversation.

The awareness of the significance of critical minerals in all aspects of our life I think that that is growing, but I do think that the legislation that we have presented before the committee here is one that will help us build on that. But the whole aspect of transparency and just how far removed throughout this chain you have the actual minerals themselves versus the application.

I think this goes exactly to what you were speaking of Senator Manchin when you asked you know from semiconductor perspective or from the perspective of the auto industry where you're getting your stuff from. Most of it is just so far removed that we just don't make that connection. We need to figure out how we better make that connection so that that risk is fully informed and with that I thank you and thank all the members of the panel here.

Senator MANCHIN. Now I will just follow up and say thank you all for attending and your insight and hopefully you can get us some information and find out exactly the effect this going to have because I truly believe with the policies we have in this country allowing foreign countries to own these vital resources that we need, and we're going to be dependent on many generations to come and basically what would effect—if we shutdown what would it effect the economics of this country.

That would be vital for us to know that if you could help us with that we'd appreciate it. I do appreciate all of your input. Does anybody have any final comments they want to make before we close this out?

If not, meetings adjourned.

[Whereupon, at 12:10 p.m., the hearing was adjourned.]

APPENDIXES

APPENDIX I

Responses to Additional Questions

RESPONSE OF DAVID ISAACS TO QUESTION FROM SENATOR WYDEN

Question 1. As the Committee learned from the helium situation, the supply of raw materials to manufacturing industries like yours doesn't get a lot of national attention until suddenly you don't have them. Like helium, there really aren't a lot of substitutes for some of these critical minerals in the manufacturing process; but unlike helium, the specific minerals that are critical vary from industry to industry. What's the best approach to make sure that Federal Government is working closely with industries like yours to make sure that our efforts are focused on the right minerals and processing and manufacturing processes?

Answer. We believe that close consultation between government and industry will be essential in identifying the right critical minerals and the appropriate policies needed to avoid future supply disruptions. We recommend that the government should actively engage with a wide range of industry sectors and solicit the views of industry experts in materials and supply chain management on these matters. As stated in our testimony, the semiconductor industry would welcome the opportunity to engage with the appropriate government officials on this issue. Accordingly, the government should establish a forum for a structured dialogue with industry experts, perhaps in the form of an advisory committee or similar entity.

In addition, it will be critical to ensure that the list of critical minerals remains current and is adjusted in response to changing circumstances, so the consultation between government and industry must happen on an ongoing basis. In this regard, we note that Section 101(e)(1) of the Critical Minerals Policy Act (S.1600) provides that the list of critical minerals should be reviewed and updated every 5 years. The dialogue between government and industry should be integrated as part of this process.

RESPONSE OF DAVID ISAACS TO QUESTION FROM SENATOR BARRASSO

Question 1. In your testimony, you discuss the importance of helium to semiconductor manufacturers. You explain that S. 1600's definition of "critical mineral" might not include helium. You note that helium is a byproduct of natural gas and that the bill's definition of "critical mineral" excludes: "fuel minerals, including . . . natural gas." You go on to say that: "the bill should be broad enough and flexible enough to trigger appropriate revisions to policies relating to helium.

Would you please elaborate on why it is essential that the bill address helium and policies associated with helium production?

Answer. SIA believes that the enactment into law of the Helium Stewardship Act was critical in ensuring a continued supply of this critical gas to the semiconductor industry and other users of helium throughout the economy. Passage of the helium law last year successfully addressed concerns about the supply of helium, at least for the next several years. The SIA testimony did not intend to focus solely on helium or suggest that this bill should address policies related to helium. Instead, our intent was to use helium as an example and urge the Committee to ensure that the bill would cover the full range of materials that are critical to semiconductor manufacturing, in order to avoid future supply disruptions and price with regard to other materials. The SIA testimony raised the potential for helium and other similar materials to fall outside the definition of "critical mineral," and stated:

There may be other materials or compounds that are essential to the semiconductor manufacturing process that might inadvertently fall outside the definition of this term. Accordingly, we request that the definition of "critical mineral" (or "critical material") is broad enough to capture the full range of materials that are critical to semiconductor manufacturing and the U.S. economy as a whole.

Similarly, our testimony stated that the designation of a material as critical should result in consideration of a broad range of policy changes to avoid potential disruptions to the supply of this material, not simply policies relating to mining. Our reference to the Helium Stewardship Act was intended as an example of one such policy change that should be contemplated in the future once a material is designated as critical. We did not intend to suggest that the Critical Minerals Policy Act needed to revisit the Helium Stewardship Act at this time.

RESPONSES OF ROBERT H. LATIFF TO QUESTIONS FROM SENATOR WYDEN

Question 1. Although the Committee on Energy and Natural Resources doesn't have jurisdiction over the defense agencies, Sen. Murkowski and I recognize the need to make sure that national security is part of a national program to address critical minerals. What are your recommendations to ensure that defense agencies are working closely with civilian agencies like the Department of Energy and the Department of Interior on this problem?

Answer. I know that in developing the annual stockpile reports to Congress, DLA (DOD) coordinates with Dept. of Commerce on usage rates of various materials. I think that research portfolios, while not necessarily de-conflicted, are at least shared, say between DOD and DOE, on these topics. I think there is evidence of coordination at many levels and on many topics. The Defense Production Act Committee is an example. Such high level committees have numerous working level groups below them. However, in my experience, agencies, lacking any higher level of guidance, while willing to coordinate, will tend to protect organizational equities. There really needs to be active and sustained involvement by the Executive Office of the President and OMB. While not precisely associated with this question, I think the President's Initiatives for Advanced Manufacturing and for the Materials Genome Initiative are related, and are steps in the right direction. These are emphasized from the top of the Executive Branch to all appropriate agencies. A similar Presidential priority placed on materials security, in the form of a "Critical Materials Availability Initiative" would be a welcome counterpart to S. 1600. Also, perhaps, an annual report to Congress by the Director of the Office of Science and Technology Policy (OSTP) might spur more sustained efforts by all agencies.

Question 2. Although there is obviously a strong connection between critical minerals and national security, the use of those minerals is generally known. Do you see any reason why the list of critical minerals should be classified and not available to the public?

Answer. As you know, the DOD conducts scenario planning in its effort to determine what materials may be critical and in short supply under certain conflict conditions. Based on those analyses, DOD reports to Congress what it believes might need to be stockpiled in the event of future wartime scenarios. While unlikely, the DOD, so as not to reveal strategic thinking on particular conflict scenarios, may have good reasons to classify such a report to Congress. However, the overall determination on an ongoing basis for those materials important to us and for which the nation needs to take action to insure their availability, should be widely known. I see absolutely no reason for such a list of critical materials to be classified. On the contrary, it needs to be open and available and act as a guiding document.

Question 3. One of the key tenants of a strong military has always been to stay ahead of the opposition technologically. As you point out in your testimony, critical minerals are literally critical to national security since so many of our weapons systems rely on them. Recently, the Defense Authorization Bill called on the Pentagon to increase its stockpiles of critical minerals. That might be a short-term solution to the problem, but wouldn't you agree that in the long-term, the U.S. has to have a more comprehensive strategy toward dealing with this problem?

Answer. I absolutely agree with this sentiment. In general, I think the DOD has made significant progress in the last several years in thinking about and trying to deal with these issues. There have been substantial improvements in DLA's methodologies to address the stockpile needs, there has been the creation of the Strategic Materials Protection Board (albeit off to a slow start), and I think there have been a lot of dedicated materials experts at lower levels within the Department who have recognized problems of resource dependency and have worked steadily to mitigate them. However, I think DOD leadership has been slow to react and it is still not clear to me that DOD has coherent plans beyond stockpiling a few key materials and supporting Defense Production Act projects for some key suppliers. Stockpiling is a short-term fix and is subject to many variables. It doesn't solve the problem of having to depend on others for either raw materials, materials processing, or component manufacturing for which we may not have the domestic capability. I would like to see a more coherent approach to working with other government agencies to insure domestic supplies and processing capabilities for the most important materials.

RESPONSE OF JENNIFER THOMAS TO QUESTION FROM SENATOR WYDEN

Question 1. As the Committee learned from the helium situation, the supply of raw materials to manufacturing industries like yours doesn't get a lot of national attention until suddenly you don't have them. Like helium, there really aren't a lot of substitutes for some of these critical minerals in the manufacturing process; but unlike helium, the specific minerals that are critical vary from industry to industry. What's the best way to make sure that Federal Government is working closely with industries like yours to make sure that our efforts are focused on the right minerals and processing and manufacturing processes?

Answer. The Alliance appreciates the opportunity to provide input on ways the Federal Government and industry can work together on the very important issue of critical mineral availability. Automakers design and build vehicles to synthesize a variety of systems and individual parts to meet an array of individual customer needs and demands and to comply with thousands of pages of international, federal and state regulations. The average automobile has 30,000 unique components and each individual component is comprised of multiple chemicals, minerals and mixtures. Each automaker works with a global network of more than 1,000 suppliers, spanning multiple sectors from electronics to textiles. Many automotive components are obtained from suppliers as finished products, which are then integrated into the vehicle. As such, it is essential that any coordination on the issue of critical mineral availability and processing begin at the supplier level, where component composition decisions are made.

Many policies outlined in S.1600, the Critical Minerals Policy Act will help spur much-needed cooperation between government and industry on this important issue. For example, this legislation will establish analytical and forecasting capabilities to better identify critical mineral supply and demand. This will help mitigate supply shortages, price volatility, and unexpected demand growth. Such analysis and forecasting for minerals, similar to what the U.S. Energy Information Administration (EIA) produces for various energy sources, will help industry identify potential risks early and ultimately manage them. Additionally, the Department of Energy (DOE) research programs created in S.1600 would facilitate the efficient production, use and recycling of critical minerals. These programs would also identify and develop alternative materials that can be used to reduce the demand of critical minerals. To effectively implement such programs, the Alliance recommends that DOE coordinate closely with the diverse stakeholders in order to develop best practices and innovative approaches for using existing minerals more efficiently and for introducing viable and affordable alternatives when necessary.

The Alliance commends the Committee for the thoughtful and bipartisan approach it has taken to address this important policy issue. Minerals have long been vital to automobile production and the more sophisticated, high-tech and fuel-efficient automobiles of tomorrow will be increasingly reliant on critical minerals. We stand ready to work with the Committee to ensure a reliable and affordable critical minerals market.

RESPONSE OF JIM SIMS TO QUESTION FROM SENATOR BARRASSO

Question 1a. In your testimony, you state that Molycorp: "walked a regulatory pathway that took 15 years and more than 500 permits to restart rare earth production in California." You explain that: "[i]ncreased regulatory certainty is a must if the U.S. is to encourage greater private sector investment in domestic mineral exploration." You note that S. 1600: "recognizes that much can be done to make permitting processes more efficient." Finally, you say that the bill: "should spark new thinking and innovative ideas for reasonable reforms." What are the additional steps Congress should take to expedite the permitting process for critical minerals projects?

Answer. There are a variety of pathways that the U.S. Government can take to make these processes more efficient. Perhaps one of the most important would be to require/encourage/incentivize applicants and federal agencies to work together on concurrent permit reviews under NEPA, rather than the consecutive reviews that are generally done now. That would save all parties a great deal of time and resources.

Requiring publicly available performance metrics of federal agency actions and review of permits would be a very significant reform. This would allow officials from both political parties to look dispassionately at the relative efficiency of these government processes. It also is likely to identify areas where improvements can and should be made.

Also, thought should be given to requiring disclosure of the various economic and societal costs of inaction, or delay, in permitting processes. This might be a contentious proposal, but it would provide policymakers and the public with additional information to consider in the debate that often surrounds individual critical materials projects.

Question 1b. Should Congress take steps to expedite the review process under the National Environmental Policy Act?

Answer. NEPA processes can undoubtedly be improved, as can virtually all federal statutes of this complexity and impact on the economy and the environment. However, any such reforms should be the result of a legislative process that includes buy-in from both political parties. While this is very difficult, attempts to push through NEPA reforms without some level of bipartisan cooperation are doomed to failure, in my view, and can actually set back the overall thrust to greater efficiency. This is why I believe that S. 1600 is a good step forward, given that it may shed important light on data and trends that would better inform future debates on the larger permitting regime.

RESPONSE OF RODERICK EGGERT TO QUESTION FROM SENATOR WYDEN

Question 1. Colorado School of Mines is one of the few schools in the country with academic classes and programs focused on critical minerals, and you've been teaching there for over 25 years. General Latiff's testimony says essentially that the number of technical papers and the number of people being trained in these disciplines are dropping compared to the rest of the world. The U.S. isn't keeping up. What are the training and education needs that must be met in order to have a workforce that is prepared to operate within a more robust critical material industry?

Answer. The primary needs are in the following areas: economic geology, mining engineering, mineral processing and extractive metallurgy, and materials science and engineering. Perhaps just as important are (funded) research opportunities that attract faculty members and students in more traditional disciplines to research on critical materials (for example, chemistry, chemical engineering, and physics).

RESPONSES OF RODERICK EGGERT TO QUESTIONS FROM SENATOR BARRASSO

Question 1A. In your testimony, you say that we should "[i]mprove [the] regulatory-approval processes for domestic resource development." You explain that the approval process: "is costly and time consuming-arguably excessively so, not just for mines but for developments in all sectors of the economy." Finally, you state that S. 1600 would be "an important start to improving the efficiency" of the regulatory approval process. Would you please elaborate on how the regulatory approval process is far too costly and time-consuming to mineral producers?

Answer. A major issue, perhaps the most important issue, is the number of permits and approvals required and the lack of an orderly process to coordinate applications and reviews of applications. Other countries, such as Australia and Canada, are able to achieve comparable or better results, in terms of allowing for public participation and incorporating public views into regulatory reviews, with simpler and less-cumbersome processes.

Question 1B. To what extent does the National Environmental Policy Act (NEPA) contribute to these excessive costs and delays?

Answer. I do not feel qualified to comment specifically on NEPA.

Question 1C. Should Congress take steps to expedite the review process under NEPA?

Answer. Again, I do not feel qualified to suggest specific modifications to NEPA.

Question 2. In your testimony, you argue that the United States should: "[e]ncourage undistorted international trade." You explain that: "raw material-importing nations should fight policies of exporting countries that restrict raw material exports." You note that the U.S., Europe, and Japan have fought China's export restrictions on critical minerals at the World Trade Organization.

Over the last year, this Committee has debated the costs and benefits of exporting liquefied natural gas (LNG). The Committee will soon debate the costs and benefits of exporting crude oil.

Isn't it fair to say that our nation's own restrictions on LNG and crude oil exports undermine our credibility when advocating for free trade of other raw materials-such as critical minerals?

Answer. I do not support restrictions on LNG and crude oil exports.

RESPONSE OF RODERICK EGGERT TO QUESTION FROM SENATOR FRANKEN

Question 1. Critical minerals are essential for a wide range of technologies today. But technology, as you know, is changing rapidly. My concern is that figuring out which minerals will be critical in the future is difficult, particularly for rapidly evolving high-tech applications. How can we ensure that the process for designating minerals as "critical minerals" is flexible enough to take into account the potential for future changes to which minerals are actually critical?

Answer. (1) I agree that figuring out which materials may become critical in the future is difficult and will not become an exact science. The process of monitoring potentially critical materials inevitably will require judgment, as well as attention to technological developments that may dramatically influence demand for specific elements and materials. What I suggest is a continuing monitoring capability to reduce the likelihood of being surprised, which is what happened with rare-earth elements.

(2) More specifically, establishing an external advisory or review board with rotating membership, responsible for reviewing and vetting draft lists of critical minerals, would help ensure that new viewpoints are considered by whomever in the federal government is responsible for undertaking identification of critical minerals.

RESPONSES OF DAVID DANIELSON TO QUESTIONS FROM SENATOR MURKOWSKI

Question 1. Many of us look to the Department of Energy to be an advocate for our energy supply within the councils of our government. There's a corollary concern present here, however: because so many new energy technologies rely so heavy on critical minerals, we also need your Department to be an advocate for our domestic mineral supply. Can you make that commitment to us? In the interagency process, are you willing to highlight the importance of, and push for actions that would facilitate, a steady, affordable, and domestic supply of minerals?

Answer. The Department is committed to ensuring a sustainable domestic supply chain for the clean energy economy, including the foundational materials supporting clean energy technologies. The Department's Critical Materials Strategy reports make clear that diversified global supply chains are essential for a sustainable clean energy economy.

The Critical Materials Institute (CMI) at Ames National Laboratory is a lead contributor to the Department's research and development on critical materials issues. CMI addresses materials criticality problems by developing technologies spanning the supply chain and across the lifecycle of materials.

DOE takes an active role in interagency coordination, collaboration, and planning in the critical materials space to help the U.S. government make better strategic decisions, and will continue interagency leadership as co-chair of the National Science and Technology Council Subcommittee on Critical and Strategic Mineral Supply Chains. This Subcommittee facilitates a strong, coordinated effort across federal agencies to identify and address important policy implications arising from strategic minerals supply issues. Areas of focus for the Subcommittee include identifying emerging critical materials, improving depth ofinformation, and identifying R&D priorities. The Subcommittee also informally reviews and examines domestic and global policies that affect the supply of critical materials, such as permitting, export restrictions, recycling, and stockpiling.

Question 2. Is the Department working on any follow-up reports to supplement its 2010 and 2011 Critical Mineral Strategy documents? If so, please describe the expected timing of their release and the expected scope of their content.

Answer. By the end of2014, the Department of Energy plans to assess whether an update to the 2011 Critical Materials Strategy is needed, given the related research and development and coordination work underway.

In addition to the Critical Materials Strategy reports, the Department of the Interior, through the USGS Mineral Resources Program, provides annual collection, analysis, and the dissemination of data that document production and consumption for about 100 mineral commodities, both domestically and internationally for 180 countries (http://minerals.usgs.gov/minerals). This full spectrum of mineral resource science allows for a comprehensive understanding of the complete life cycle of nonfuel mineral resources-resource formation, discovery, production, consumption, use, recycling and reuse.

Question 3. The Department has allocated hundreds of millions of taxpayer dollars to develop high-density energy storage devices that utilize lithium metal. Yet global demand for lithium is rising, particularly in China, and the United States is already heavily dependent on imports. Has the Department analyzed any potential supply chain impacts that we could face with regard to lithium? Could we see a situation similar to what has happened with rare earth elements? How could that impact our ability to commercialize new technologies that rely upon this metal?

Answer. In 2010 and 2011, the Department released Critical Materials Strategy reports which, in addition to identifying critical materials, identified lithium as a "near critical" material. The reports identified lithium because of its important role in batteries for hybrid and electric vehicles. While lithium does not face the same magnitude of risk to supply chain disruption as rare earth elements, the Department is still applying the three pillars of the Critical Materials Strategy to lithium research and development.

The Department is currently addressing this issue by reducing criticality risks for lithium. Because of the projected importance of lithium supply for clean energy applications, the Department will continue R&D in this important area to mitigate potential supply chain constraints. For example, within the Office of Energy Efficiency and Renewable Energy the Geothermal Technologies Office has funded the development of technologies to cost effectively extract minerals such as lithium, manganese and zinc from geothermal brines- to improve domestic production at reduced costs and to increase the overall value of geothermal electricity generation. The Vehicle Technologies Office has supported a project to expand lithium carbonate and lithium hydroxide production to supply the domestic battery industry as well as a project to recycle lithium batteries for resale of lithium carbonate.

Question 4. Given the range of new technologies that are expected to account for larger and larger shares of lithium consumption, does the Department believe we could face constraints or even a shortage in the supply of lithium available for more traditional applications such as batteries? Has the Department done anything to help mitigate such a scenario? What steps, if any, does the Department believe are warranted to prevent that from happening?

Answer. As mentioned above, the Department is addressing potential supply constraints with regard to lithium. Currently, the Department's research efforts focus on diversifying supply, developing substitutes, and driving recycling of lithium. Because there are significant additional low cost potential sources of lithium from desert brines, lithium has a lower risk of supply disruption than certain rare earth elements, even under high global electric vehicle deployment scenarios. However, because dramatic increase in global lithium battery production could lead to asupply-demand mismatch in the next five years, the Department is applying the three pillars of the Critical Materials Strategy to lithium research and development.

The Critical Materials Institute at Ames National Laboratory conducts research and development (R&D) addressing supply diversity, substitutes, and recycling for lithium. Other national laboratories also contribute to lithium R&D. For example, the Joint Center for Energy Storage Research (JCESR), the Energy Innovation Hub for Battery and Energy Storage, is addressing lithium substitutes. Launched in December 2012, JCESR is managed by the Department's Office of Science and is led by Argonne National Laboratory. The mission of JCESR is to develop new battery chemistries beyond lithium-ion and to deliver electrical energy storage with five times the energy density and one-fifth the cost oftoday's commercial batteries within five years.

Within the Office of Energy Efficiency and Renewable Energy, the Vehicles Technology Office has supported a project to expand lithium carbonate and lithium hydroxide production to supply the domestic battery industry, and the Geothermal Technologies Office has funded the development of technologies to cost effectively extract minerals such as lithium from geothermal brines to improve domestic production at reduced costs and to increase the overall value of geothermal electricity generation.

Finally, the Department's Advanced Research Projects Agency- Energy also supports R&D on a broad array of novel battery technologies that do not use the lithium-ion platform.

RESPONSES OF DAVID DANIELSON TO QUESTIONS FROM SENATOR FRANKEN

Question 1. Rare earths are critical to the high-tech sector and the energy sector. But in many cases, we are dependent on imports from China. In recent years, we've seen large price increases for these rare earth elements, and we need to make sure that our dependency doesn't harm our manufacturing sector. This is one of the reasons why I am a cosponsor of S. 1600, the Critical Minerals Policy Act of 2013. Can you talk about which particular clean energy technologies are most dependent on rare earth elements?

Answer. The Department's 2010 and 2011 Critical Materials Strategy reports identified five rare earth materials-neodymium, europium, terbium, dysprosium, and yttrium- as critical materials currently essential for America's transition to cost-competitive clean energy technologies and subject to supply risk. Neodymium and dysprosium are used for magnets, which are found in electric vehicle motors and wind turbine generators. Europium, terbium, and yttrium are used in phosphors for efficient lighting. In addition, another rare earth element, lanthanum, is used in nickel metal hydride batteries. However, as lanthanum is relatively abundant, DOE did not identify it as critical in its Critical Materials Strategy reports.

Question 2. How does our dependence on China impact these sectors of the clean energy economy?

Answer. While China has been and continues to be a dominant source for critical materials, the on-going challenge is developing a secure domestic supply chain or substitutes for these critical materials so that as clean energy technologies are developed and deployed in the United States they can also be manufactured in the United States. The vulnerability associated with global dependence on critical materials underscores the importance of the Department's research and development activities in this area. The Department's Critical Materials Strategy and coordinated R&D efforts address supply chain disruption risks by diversifying supply, developing substitutes, and driving recycling of critical materials.

Question 3. What have been the major barriers that have prevented us from mining, separating, and refining rare earth elements for use here in the United States?

Answer. One of the primary barriers to upstream domestic critical materials development has been the high capital requirements associated with overcoming the technical challenges at this stage in the supply chain. This barrier to entry has led to a natural monopoly of processing operations concentrated in certain countries.

The Department addresses processing innovations through research and development (R&D) to help reduce processing capital requirements. For example, the Critical Materials Institute is considering new, lower cost ways to extract, separate, and process rare earth metals from ores and recycled materials, such as neodymium for permanent magnets and europium for lighting.

APPENDIX II

Additional Material Submitted for the Record

STATEMENT OF DR. JOHN G. PARRISH, CHAIR (AASG), CALIFORNIA GEOLOGICAL SURVEY, DEPARTMENT OF CONSERVATION, SACRAMENTO, CA

Thank you for the opportunity to submit written testimony for the record on S. 1600, the Critical Minerals Policy Act of 2013. This testimony is presented on behalf of the Association of American State Geologists (AASG). Our organization represents the State Geologists of the 50 United States and Puerto Rico. Founded in 1908, AASG seeks to advance the science and practical application of geology and related earth sciences in the United States and its territories, commonwealths, and possessions. AASG strives to optimize the role that State Geological Survey agencies play in delivering benefits to the people of the United States in relation to developing economic prosperity, understanding and mitigating natural hazards, protecting the public's property and lives, as well as appreciation and preservation of our natural environmental heritage.

AASG recognizes the hard work of Chairman Wyden, Ranking Member Murkowski, the cosponsors of the Critical Minerals Act of 2013, and the members of this Committee. We commend your efforts to strengthen our nation's capacity to address the challenges associated with critical minerals and we would like to emphasize the role that State Geological Surveys can play in tackling this important issue.

AASG POSITION STATEMENT ON MINERAL RESOURCES

AASG strongly supports adequate funding of mineral resources programs within relevant Federal agencies, including the Departments of Agriculture, Defense, Energy, Health and Human Services, Interior, and Labor. Further, AASG advocates that, as appropriate, these programs be implemented through Federal-State partnerships to achieve mutually beneficial goals relative to mineral resources.

BACKGROUND

Minerals and mineral materials provide the fundamental components for manufactured goods, agricultural fertilizers, and construction. The U.S. economy, defense systems, and our lifestyle depend on stable supplies of minerals. Mineral resources are commercially quarried or mined in every state in the United States. Crushed stone, sand and gravel, needed for concrete and asphalt, are widely distributed, but many other commodities have been concentrated by geological processes and occur only in certain locations. With its large land area and diverse geological settings, the United States has many key mineral resources necessary for society to function. The locations of mineral resources are not all known.

Recent discoveries of world-class deposits of gold, copper, and zinc in the United States and continued exploration by mining companies illustrate that the U.S. remains a prime target for new mineral resource discovery.

Two studies by the National Research Council, Minerals, Critical Minerals, and the U.S. Economy, and Managing Materials for a 21st Century Military, and a 2011 report by the American Physical Society on Energy Critical Elements, find that the United States lacks sufficient information about its mineral needs and supplies. Up-to-date, accurate, geological mapping is critical to fulfilling State and Federal responsibilities for stewardship of our natural resources. Geologic maps and investigations are essential to an understanding of natural processes responsible for the formation of mineral deposits and the hydrological-chemical consequences of mining and land reclamation.

State Geological Surveys are uniquely positioned to help address the need for geological maps and studies, and to collect, preserve, and disseminate the geological information that is needed to ensure adequate domestic supplies of critical minerals.

S. 1600, THE CRITICAL MINERALS ACT OF 2013

AASG strongly supports adequately funded mineral resources programs within the relevant Federal agencies and we support the aims and actions outlined in Sections 101 (methodology for identifying critical minerals), 103 (resource assessment), 108 (analysis and forecasting), and 109 (education and workforce) of S. 1600.

We urge you to recognize the specific expertise of State Geological Surveys and to consider the following items:

Establish a grant program in strategic and critical mineral resources similar to the National Cooperative Geologic Mapping Program (NCGMP). The NCGMP, which was established under the National Geologic Mapping Act of 1992, is the primary source of funds for the production of geological maps in the United States. For over two decades, funds from the NCGMP have supported cooperation between Federal, State, and university partners to deliver modern geological maps. The maps produced under this program are one of the most valuable tools for assessing the mineral wealth and mineral potential of the nation. We urge you to consider creating a parallel program to enable effective cooperation between Federal, State, and university experts on understanding strategic and critical mineral resources.

Amend the National Geological and Geophysical Data Preservation Program Act of 2005 (42 USC 15908) to specifically mention and authorize funding for maintaining information on critical minerals. State Geological Surveys and other organizations, including Federal agencies, already hold information, such as written records, maps, drill core, rock samples, and exploration and mining records, that relate to critical minerals. These collections reflect substantial investments by industry and government over more than 150 years, yet these irreplaceable records are currently at risk of disposal or ruin because more than 25 percent of the nation's geological data repositories are currently at or near their storage capacity. Dedicating funds to preserving and providing access to existing information on critical minerals would be highly cost effective and would provide on-demand access to a trove of valuable information.

Thank you for the opportunity to present this testimony to the Committee.

STATEMENT OF INTERSTATE MINING COMPACT COMMISSION, ON S. 1600

The Interstate Mining Compact Commission (IMCC) submits this statement in support of S. 1600, The Critical Minerals Act of 2013. IMCC is a multi-state governmental agency representing the natural resource and related environmental protection interest of its 26 member states. The Commission is comprised of duly appointed representatives of the Governors of their respective departments of Natural Resources or Environmental Protection. As such, the member states ofiMCC have a vital interest in the development of minerals, particularly those of strategic and critical importance to the United States. Furthermore, one of IMCC's primary functions is to support effective communication and collaboration between our member state regulators and their counterparts in the federal agencies, especially where it pertains to permitting for mineral extraction and related activities. In pursuit of both these goals, IMCC believes that this bill will have a significant benefit and therefore lends its full support.

In the face of growing "resource nationalism" abroad, it is crucial that the US take steps to account for, protect, and further bolster domestic sources of critical minerals. Developing our Nation's mineral wealth in a manner that maximizes access while maintaining environmental responsibility must be a fundamental component of efforts to shore up national mineral resource security. One of the strategies employed by S. 1600 in pursuit of that goal is the streamlining of supply chains through elimination of unnecessary permitting requirements. Parallel permitting requirements convolute these supply chains, reducing our Nation's access to domestic sources of vitally important natural resources to the ultimate detriment of national resource security. The US should endeavor to realize the immense benefits potentially derived from intentional, conscientious development of our Nation's rich supply of mineral resources, both on state and federal lands. IMCC believes S. 1600 to be a significant step in the right direction.

In addition to the interest in enhancing our states' and thus our Nation's mineral wealth, IMCC member states have a more specific interest in supporting S. 1600. As primary regulators of mineral production activity within their borders, designing efficient but responsible permitting processes is a top priority. Even where minerals are produced on federal lands, the states often work in concert with various federal agencies in regulating minerals under applicable federal laws. Arriving at the optimal design for these often interrelated permitting processes is contingent on real and frequent collaboration among state and federal agencies. IMCC is therefore particularly supportive of provisions in S. 1600 designed to enhance this vitally important coordination. Through these collaborative efforts, state and federal agencies will hopefully be able to eliminate some of the redundant permitting and processing mechanisms currently in place in certain arenas. As Sections 102(a)(9) and 105(a)(3)(C) of the bill indicate, parallel permitting requirements lead to duplicative efforts on the part of our member state regulators and our federal colleagues. Expediting these permitting processes by minimizing unnecessary delays, preventing unnecessary paperwork, and avoiding duplication of effort, will allow all those involved to work smarter rather than harder. This in turn contributes to the ultimate goal of mineral regulation: to ensure that these resources are mined in an efficient and effective manner while also protecting the environment.

For all of these reasons, IMCC urges the Subcommittee to move forward with markup and passage of S. 1600, the Critical Minerals Policy Act of 2013. We welcome the opportunity to work with the Subcommittee and contribute to this legislative initiative and thank you for the opportunity to submit this statement. We would be happy to answer any questions or provide additional information.

STATEMENT OF MATERIOR CORPORATION, MAYFIELD HEIGHTS, OH, ON S. 1600

The Materion Corporation (Materion), headquartered in Mayfield Heights, Ohio, respectfully submits the following comments to the United States Senate Committee on Energy and Natural Resources regarding S. 1600, the Critical Minerals Policy Act of 2013.

Materion supplies highly engineered advanced enabling materials to leading and dynamic technology companies across the globe. Our product offerings include precious and non-precious specialty metals, precision optical filters, inorganic chemicals and powders, specialty coatings and engineered clad and plated metal systems.

Our products, services and expertise help enable our customers' technologies. We supply sophisticated thin film coatings for hard disk drives, specialty inorganic chemicals for solar energy panels, bio-compatible materials for implantable medical devices, specialty alloys for miniature consumer electronics components, optical filters for thermal imaging, critical components for infrared sensing technology, special materials for LEDs and much more.

Materion is the free-world's only integrated "mine-to-mill" supplier of beryllium-based products. Materion owns and operates its beryllium mine in Delta, Utah, and has characterized a 70+year supply of beryllium ore. Small deposits of beryllium ore are found in Kazakhstan and China, but Materion mines in excess of 70 percent of the world's supply. Currently, China does not export its supply of beryllium.

Beryllium is a metallic element that has extremely unique properties. To name just a few, it is onethird lighter than aluminum, has six times the specific stiffness of steel and is transparent to X-rays. Adding up to 2 percent beryllium to copper imparts springiness comparable to steel and corrosion resistance like stainless steel, yet retaining the electrical and thermal conductivity properties of copper. For these and other reasons, beryllium is the only material to be defined by the U.S. Department of Defense (DoD) as both strategic and critical to the United States. Beryllium is also defined as a critical material by the European Commission.

Beryllium materials are used in research and industrial applications where reliability and superior performance are required. The final seal capping the leaking oil well in the Gulf of Mexico was a large ring of copper beryllium. The James Webb Space Telescope, launching this decade, has 16 beryllium mirrors to capture the images from space. The 2012 Nobel Peace prize for physics used atoms of beryllium to create a computer chip with the computing capacity of every computer on earth today. In short, beryllium can do things that no other element on earth can do.

Materion offers the following comments on S. 1600, the Critical Minerals Policy Act of 2013.

1. Materion strongly supports developing a critical minerals policy as US leadership in innovation and technology is inextricably linked to reliable access to and use of critical minerals.

As stated, the intent of S. 1600 is, "To facilitate the reestablishment of domestic, critical mineral designation, assessment, production, manufacturing, recycling, analysis, forecasting, workforce, education, research, and international capabilities in the United States, and for other purposes."

As a producer and key supplier of critical materials, Materion sees great value in US policies that would strengthen both domestic capabilities and international trade to ensure adequate supply of these materials. Materion supports these goals.

2. Beryllium should be designated as a critical mineral under the provisions of the Critical Minerals Policy Act of 2013.

According to the text of S. 1600, the Secretary of Interior is directed to develop a draft methodology for assessing and determining a list of not more than 20 critical minerals. The methodology would be published in the Federal Register for notice and comment. The assessment would be based on potential international supply restrictions and the importance of use, including energy technologies, defense, agriculture, consumer electronics and health carerelated applications.

This limited interpretation of what would constitute a critical mineral under the bill and in the implementing regulations may disqualify beryllium even though it is of critical importance for use and innovation in the energy, defense, consumer electronics and health care marketplace. Beryllium should not be penalized by a designation protocol because Materion has worked hard to ensure an adequate long-term supply.

Unnecessary over-regulation of beryllium is the greatest threat to the key markets for beryllium and the future sustainability of a US supply. Worldwide supply of beryllium to the free world comes primarily from a single source in the US—Materion. Small deposits of beryllium ore are found in Kazakhstan and China, but Materion mines in excess of 70 percent of the world's supply. China does not export its supply of beryllium. The company estimates a 70+year supply of beryllium ore.

Since beryllium ore is mined and processed domestically, the primary current threat to US supply is not due to foreign trading partners restricting imports of this critical mineral into the US. Rather, unnecessary over-regulation of beryllium is the greatest threat to the key markets for beryllium and the future sustainability of a US supply. Regulatory overreach has the potential to disrupt the beryllium business balance that enables Materion to supply strategic and critical applications of this mineral for defense and commercial customers. If US production becomes infeasible due to US or foreign regulatory policies, the US could be held hostage by China or Kazakhstan who would not be able to meet world demands. A constrained supply of beryllium for the US would very likely follow the pattern that has occurred with other critical minerals; e.g., rare earths and China domination.

3. Notwithstanding the potential definitional restriction of a critical mineral under S. 1600, the US Department of Defense (DoD) has determined beryllium to be the only strategic and critical material for US national security.

See: (Report required by Section 843 of Public Law 109-364: Report of Meeting, Department of Defense, Strategic Materials Protection Board, December 12, 2008). DoD's determination is based on the fact that:

> High purity beryllium is both a strategic and critical material.
>
> High purity beryllium is essential for important defense systems, and it is unique in the function it performs. High purity beryllium possesses unique properties that make it indispensable in many of today's critical U.S. defense systems, including sensors, missiles and satellites, avionics, and nuclear weapons.
>
> There is significant risk of supply disruption. Without DoD involvement and support, U.S. industry would not be able to provide the materials for defense applications. There are no reliable foreign suppliers that could provide high purity beryllium to the Department.

DoD stated, " . . . beryllium meets all the conditions for being a critical material," and concluded, "the Department should continue to take those special actions necessary to maintain a long term domestic supply of high purity beryllium." (emphasis added) Those special actions included the U.S. government investing $80+ million in a Title III Defense Production Act project with Materion to ensure a reliable supply of beryllium in the US.

A 2013 Rand Corporation report, Critical Materials, Present Danger to U.S. Manufacturing, identified beryllium as a highly concentrated critical material although primary production is in the US.

The Senate Committee on Energy and Natural Resources should include provisions in S. 1600 specifically designating materials deemed strategic and critical to DoD as a critical mineral to align with US national security interests.

4. The European Union (EU) has also designated beryllium as a critical material and has publically expressed concerns on the impacts of over regulation of beryllium, in key emerging technologies in the electronics industry.

The European Commission (EC) listed beryllium as one of fourteen critical materials (European Commission Critical Raw Materials for the EU—Report of the Ad-hoc Working Group on defining critical raw materials, 2010). Raw materials are designated as being "critical" when the risks for supply shortage and their impacts on the economy are higher compared to other raw materials.

According to the EC paper,

> The most significant threats originate from perceived risks associated with the use of beryllium in electronic products. EU regulatory fears and NGO-propagated "banning" of the use of materials containing beryllium lead to unwarranted attempts to find substitutes that do not offer the same qualities with respect to performance, sustainability and environmental protection. The data that authorities rely on is not current and does not reflect the most recent scientific studies. In general, authorities are reluctant to break from the past and are not open to new scientific studies even if they are conducted in accord with OECD guidelines or originate from proven workplace strategies. Because the cost of beryllium is high compared with that of other materials, it is used in applications in which its properties are crucial. In some applications, certain metal matrix or organic composites, high-strength grades of aluminum, pyrolytic graphite, silicon carbide, steel, or titanium may be substituted for beryllium metal or beryllium composites. Copper alloys containing nickel and silicon, tin, titanium, or other alloying elements or phosphor bronze alloys (copper-tin-phosphorus) may be substituted for beryllium-copper alloys, but these substitutions can result in substantially reduced performance.

5. Materion offers the following recommendations to revise S. 1600 for the Committee's consideration.

Materion urges the Committee to carefully craft the criteria for designation of a critical mineral in S. 1600 by giving greater weight to the criticality of a mineral versus its current supply limitations. Supply limitations come and go with market demands and, therefore, there is no basis for over-weighting supply in the designation criteria. Minerals deemed both strategic and critical to US national security interests should be mandated for inclusion in the designation process developed by the Department of Interior. Consistency among Cabinetlevel departments regarding a concise regulatory policy for beryllium as a critical mineral is absolutely necessary. Its strategic importance to national defense and its contribution to enhanced public safety, energy independence, innovation, and unique applications that foster economic growth and job preservation warrant beryllium being designated as critical.

We recommend the following.

(a) S. 1600 should be amended to allow beryllium to be designated as a critical mineral. For any material DoD designates as strategic and critical, the Secretary of the Interior should automatically designate it as critical as well, and it should be included in the initial list of 20 substances. US national security interests should take precedence. Keep in mind that beryllium is a key material in every atomic weapon and is critical to our armed forces in its use in fighter aircraft, tanks, weapons guidance systems, night vision systems, spacecraft, and satellites. The use of beryllium not only protects those who serve our country, but also gives them a tactical advantage.

For example, a third provision could be added to Section 101 stating: "Notwithstanding the methodology to be developed by the Secretary of the Interior, any mineral deemed strategic and critical to US defense or national security is automatically designated as a critical mineral and should be included as part of the Department of the Interior's published list."

(b) For the reasons stated above, the legislation should include a provision that specifically requires the Department of the Interior to consult with the Department of Defense.

(c) Alternatively, at a minimum, the two criteria for a substance to qualify as a critical mineral in the Department of Interior methodology should be amended from an AND to an OR. [Section 101(a)(1) and (2)].

While this option may open the criteria for consideration of a much broader group of minerals, it would allow for the consideration of those minerals strategic and critical to national security that are not threatened by traditional international supply restrictions.

6. Beryllium uses are hallmarks of innovation that are only possible through critical minerals that give the US technological advantages over other countries.

Beryllium is a very unique critical mineral that provides functionality in a number of high-tech applications on which both commercial and defense customers rely. The following discussion describes many of the leading edge technology applications of the strategic and critical mineral beryllium.

Approximately 80 percent of the beryllium used goes into copper beryllium alloys, that are used to exploit an unmatched combination of physical properties to produce highly reliable components of systems that protect lives and where failure could be either life-threatening or would provide lower performance and reduced quality of life.

Copper beryllium alloys are used for the manufacture of high performance, electrically conductive terminals such as:

—Extremely reliable automobile connectors for air bag crash sensor and deployment systems, anti-lock brake systems, and new drive-by-wire technologies.
—Life-saving medical applications such as the connections in medical operating rooms and monitoring equipment.
—Critical connections and relays in electrical, electronic and telecommunications equipment where failure would disrupt the communications of emergency services like firefighters and police.
—No-fail aircraft and spacecraft electrical and electronic connectors, which enable, for example, fly-by-wire commercial airliners to achieve previously impossible fuel efficiencies.
—Household appliance temperature and other function controls that provide reliability and safety to consumers while minimizing energy and water use.
—Relays used for telephone exchanges and controlling industrial, domestic and automobile electrical equipment.

Copper beryllium alloys are used for the manufacture of mechanical components such as:

—Critical aircraft components such as altimeter diaphragms.
—Extremely long service life fire sprinkler water control valve springs that must react to fires after decades of inactivity to save lives and control fire damage.
—Non-magnetic equipment components used in oil & gas exploration, production and directional drilling equipment to improve extraction efficiencies and reduce land despoliation at drill sites by reducing the number and footprint of drill sites.
—Coal and mineral mining equipment bearings that operate longer underground.
—Mine detection and minesweeping systems that keep the global forces safe.
—Undersea fiber optic cable signal amplification "repeater" housings that carry more simultaneous transmissions than ever conceived of in the original cable systems.
—Low-friction, high-strength aircraft landing gear bearings, control rod ends and wing aileron/flap bearing bushings that allow significant weight loss to reportedly lower global fuel consumption and reduced associated carbon dioxide emissions.
—High thermal efficiency, reduced icing, aircraft components such as pitot tubes to provide enhanced aircraft safety for passengers.
—Electrode holders and components of welding robots for automated automobile and appliance welding allowing better working environments for factory workers.
—Property modifier for aluminum and magnesium castings with enhanced properties that reduce weight to achieve fuel and pollution reduction in automobiles and trucks.
—Plastic and metal casting molds with enhanced thermal efficiency.

Approximately 20 percent of the beryllium used is in the form of pure metal, as a metal matrix composite containing over 50 percent beryllium or as a beryllium oxide ceramic.

—X-ray transparent windows used to control and focus X-ray beams in all medical, scientific and analytical devices incorporating X-ray sources, providing finer resolution thereby allowing earlier cancer detection in mammography and other medical interventions.

—Gyroscope gimbals and yokes for use in guidance, navigational and targeting systems used on aircraft, armored vehicle and marine missile systems providing levels of precision that give our forces tactical advantages and minimize collateral damage.

—Satellite-mounted directional control devices for astronomical and other telescopes and instruments to provide accurate GPS locations signals and a wealth of scientific, agricultural and climatic data.

—Satellite structural components that reduce weight, provide unmatchable rigidity at deep space low temperatures and enable longer, more capable space missions.

—Mirrors for terrestrial and space-mounted astronomical telescopes that expand our knowledge of the universe, including the mirrors on the James Webb Telescope. Beryllium mirrors were not originally used on the Hubble telescope, but NASA eventually had to use small beryllium mirrors to clear up Hubble's blurred vision during a Hubble repair space mission.

—Beryllium is critical for the success of the multi-national ITER fusion energy project located in Cadaraches, France that offers the opportunity to provide sustainable energy sourced from non-radioactive nuclear fusion. Beryllium is the only material that can withstand the heat to control the fireball-like plasma inside the chamber.

—Medical isotope production nuclear reactors produce critical isotopes for treatment of many types of cancer as a result of the unique neutron beam reflective capabilities of beryllium.

—Substrates for mounting high-powered civil aviation radar systems and power amplifiers that need cooling to prevent self destruction.

—Mobile telephone infrastructure equipment.

—Medical excimer laser beam focusing and control components, allowing surgeons unprecedented fine control of the high-energy laser beam during surgery.

Preserving beryllium and other critical minerals for today's leading and life-saving technologies along with tomorrow's innovations must be a top priority to distinguish us from international competitors.

Materion thanks the Senate Energy and Natural Resources Committee for considering these comments in crafting its Critical Minerals legislation and looks forward to a continuing dialogue on this important issue. We would be pleased to meet with the Committee, and we are always available to respond to any and all questions.

STATEMENT OF DR. P. PATRICK LEAHY, CHAIR, THE MINERALS SCIENCE & INFORMATION COALITION, ON S. 1600

Thank you for the opportunity to submit written testimony on S. 1600, the Critical Minerals Policy Act of 2013, and on the importance of the federal government's mineral science and information functions.

This testimony is presented on behalf of the Minerals Science & Information Coalition (MSIC), a newly formed group of minerals and materials interests united to advocate for reinvigorated minerals science and information functions in the federal government. Initial members include the Geological Society of America, Industrial Minerals Association—North America, National Stone, Sand and Gravel Association, Society for Mining, Metallurgy, and Exploration, Inc., Portland Cement Association, National Electrical Manufacturers Association, National Mining Association, Society of Economic Geologists, and the American Geosciences Institute. Other organizations are in the process of joining the Coalition. The Coalition represents trade associations, scientific and professional societies, groups representing the extractive industries, processors, manufacturers, other mineral and material supply-chain users, and other consumers of federal minerals science and information.

MSIC commends Chairman Wyden, Ranking Member Murkowski, the cosponsors of the Critical Minerals Act of 2013, and the members of this Committee for recognizing the national importance of critical minerals and for your efforts to address this complex issue.

BACKGROUND

Minerals and mineral materials are the starting point for many supply chains that are vital to the nation's economy and national defense. Supply chains can be long, complex, and vulnerable to disruption for many reasons. This vulnerability is highlighted by recent crises in the global supply of just two commodities—rare earth elements, caused by Chinese export restrictions, and helium, caused by uncertainty surrounding the Federal Helium Reserve in Texas. Restrictions in the supply of rare earths threatened the production of components that are essential for U.S. defense and weapons systems, in addition to a vast array of communications, clean energy, electronics, automotive, and medical products. A shortage of helium threatened high-tech manufacturing, including the semiconductor industry; it also had impacts in the medical, aerospace, welding, and weather forecasting sectors. The nation's experiences with rare earth elements and helium are a wake-up call to us all.

Both the private and the public sector realize that we must reduce risk to our supply chains. But we cannot do this without accurate, timely information on the nature, location, and characteristics of our domestic mineral resources, and on the worldwide supply of, demand for, and flow of minerals and materials. This information is the foundation for identifying and forecasting existing and emerging vulnerabilities, and for sound decision making by business leaders and policy makers.

Given the vital national importance of minerals science and information, MSIC notes with alarm the consistent, severe decline in funding for the Mineral Resources Program at the U.S. Geological Survey (Fig.1)* This program is the sole federal source of scientific information and statistics on mineral resources, production, consumption, and environmental effects. The program's products are used extensively by industry, academia, policy makers, and the public, yet its funding has been cut by 30 percent, in constant dollar terms, over the past decade.

The Coalition sees a significant need for national minerals forecasting capabilities. Forecasts based on reliable information would help industry and the government to forestall and mitigate possible disruptions to the flow of essential raw materials and components and would strengthen our national resilience.

MSIC asserts that investment in minerals science, information, and forecasting is in the national interest.

S. 1600, THE CRITICAL MINERALS ACT OF 2013

We support the aims of S. 1600 to strengthen and improve our understanding of critical minerals and to develop a robust scientific and statistical information and forecasting system to identify and anticipate threats to supply chains.

In particular, the Mineral Science & Information Coalition endorses the actions proposed in Sec. 101, to develop a methodology for identifying critical minerals, Sec. 103, on resource assessments, Sec. 108, on analysis and forecasting, and Sec. 109, on education and workforce.

We urge you to continue your efforts to reinvigorate our national capacity to characterize, quantify, and forecast the sources, nature, and flow of minerals and mineral materials in support of national defense, a robust, resilient manufacturing sector, and a thriving economy.

Thank you for the opportunity to present this testimony to the Committee.

NATIONAL ELECTRICAL MANUFACTURERS ASSOCIATION,
January 31, 2014.

Hon. RON WYDEN,
Chairman, Committee on Energy and Natural Resources, Washington, DC.

Hon. LISA MURKOWSKI,
Ranking Member, Committee on Energy and Natural Resources, Washington, DC.

Re: Committee on Energy and Natural Resources Hearing on Critical Minerals Policy Act (S. 1600)

DEAR CHAIRMAN WYDEN AND RANKING MEMBER MURKOWSKI,

Thank you for the opportunity to provide the following brief remarks on behalf of the National Electrical Manufacturers Association (NEMA) on the legislation considered today by the Committee on Energy and Natural Resources: The Critical Minerals Policy Act (S. 1600).

NEMA is the association of electrical equipment and medical imaging manufacturers. Founded in 1926 and headquartered in Rosslyn, Virginia, its 400-plus member companies manufacture a diverse set of products used in the generation, transmission, distribution, and end use of electricity as well as medical diagnostic imaging. Worldwide annual sales of products in the NEMA scope exceed $140 billion.

---

* All figures have been retained in committee files.

According to the U.S Geological Survey, the U.S. was 100 percent dependent on foreign sources for 17 mineral commodities in 2012 and more than 50 percent dependent on foreign sources for some 24 more.

Challenging supply conditions and volatile prices of basic mineral inputs can be a significant threat to U.S. electroindustry companies, including in sectors such as lighting, electric motors, energy storage, superconducting materials, and medical imaging, as well as closely related industries including wind and solar electricity generation and hybrid and electric vehicles. The full scale of the threats remains uncertain, since these materials are used in various parts of product supply chains. However, while in many cases only small amounts of a specific mineral or mineral derivative may be present in a piece of manufactured equipment, its presence can be critical to performance of that equipment.

In general, NEMA supports U.S. policies that provide greater assurance to electroindustry companies of stable, continuous and affordable supplies of critical minerals. More specifically, NEMA welcomes and supports the Critical Minerals Policy Act as a multifaceted strategy to modernize U.S. federal policy on mineral resources, information, research and know-how.

The approach taken in S. 1600 is necessary to address this threat to U.S. electroindustry companies and jobs.

First, the legislation would direct the Department of the Interior to establish a methodology for determining, on an ongoing basis, the mineral resources that are most critical to the U.S. economy, including manufacturers. The methodology will be created through a public process informed by input from businesses, associations and other stakeholder organizations and will be reviewed periodically. It is our understanding that a White House chartered interagency working group has already developed a draft methodology but it has not yet been made public.

Although each company that uses minerals may have their own methods and information, the federal government plays an important role by providing objective information and guidance to policy-makers, market-makers, and other interested parties.

Second, the Act provides a set of policies across multiple federal agencies to address issues associated with the discovery, production, processing, use and re-use of critical minerals. For example, the White House is directed to establish a forecasting capability that will enable mineral policies to keep up with mineral markets and federal agencies to take steps to support economic competitiveness while maintaining environmental protections. In addition, the Interior and Agriculture Departments are tasked to ensure that federal permitting and review processes for proposed mining activities are even-handed and not stacked against well-designed and wellmanaged extraction and processing activities.

Thirdly, the legislation addresses the challenges our country faces to make better use of the mineral and human resources already at hand. Specifically, the legislation directs the Department of Energy to continue and deepen its information, research, and development activities on alternative materials and reclamation and recycling of critical minerals that have already moved through the manufacturing supply chain and have reached the end of the consumer value chain. This is of particular interest to NEMA manufacturers of fluorescent lighting products as well as equipment that employs permanent magnets. It is also important that the legislation tasks that State Department with integrating critical minerals supply chain issues into international dialogues and cooperation activities.

In addition, the legislation directs the Department of Labor to assess the portion of the U.S. workforce trained in mineral-related skills and identify present and future gaps in U.S. know-how. It also directs the Departments of Labor and Interior to collaborate in developing approaches that will enable more U.S. workers to become part of a vital U.S. minerals supply chain.

In summary, we believe the Critical Minerals Policy Act provides a comprehensive and balanced approach to updating U.S. law and policy related to minerals that are most critical for NEMA manufacturers. NEMA commends yon both for introducing this legislation and for holding the NEMA Testimony for Record of January 28, 2014 Hearing on S. 1600 Senate Committee on Energy and Natural Resources hearing of the full Committee to begin the process of moving it forward. We look forward to working with you to achieve passage by the Committee and the full Senate as soon as possible.

Thank you again for the opportunity to provide these brief remarks.

Respectfully,

KYLE PITSOR,

Vice President, Government Relations, National Electrical Manufacturers Association (NEMA).

STATEMENT OF RANDALL J. SCOTT, PRESIDENT AND CHIEF EXECUTIVE OFFICER, RARE ELEMENT, LAKEWOOD, CO

Rare Element Resources Inc. appreciates the opportunity to comment on S. 1600, "The Critical Minerals Policy Act," a bill our company strongly supports. We wish to briefly describe reasons for supporting S. 1600 and then detail why our advanced Bear Lodge Critical Rare Earths Project is poised to become America's next source of Critical Rare Earths (CREEs) by 2016.

S. 1600—We welcome the funding that S.1600 provides to improve the mineral project permitting process in the United States. Unfortunately, over the past two decades, the U.S. has become wellknown globally for imposing increasing levels of delay and uncertainty on companies that wish to create new sources of strategic and critical minerals as well as high-tech and family-wage jobs and tax revenues on American soil. In our experience, agencies such as the Forest Service, which manages the lands where our Bear Lodge Project is located, lack important resources including personnel. S. 1600 gives assurance that regulatory agencies have sufficient in-house technical staff plus sufficient funding to access competent outside experts to bolster agency talent and move permits through the National Environmental Policy Act (NEPA) process in a timely fashion.

Private capital, talent and time are precious and critical commodities in their own right. Unnecessary delays and stranded capital do nothing constructive to advance a critical rare earths project such as the Bull Hill Mine at our Bear Lodge Project toward its goal of becoming the next domestic critical rare earths producer, one that will be a strong American answer to Chinese global dominance in this sector.

Today there is a likelihood of inexplicable permitting delay that has unfortunately become the norm from federal agencies. By bringing accountability and resources to agencies doing the permitting, S. 1600 gives a greater assurance of certainty to companies such as ours that are working to meet the national goal of reestablishing a secure domestic rare earths supply chain.

In short, Rare Element Resources believes S. 1600 is a valuable and overdue step toward assurance of renewed domestic critical minerals production. Its prompt enactment will be a key factor in keeping the US competitive with our partners and a step ahead of those unfriendly to us around the world.

The Bear lodge Project—We are working to bring into production the Bear Lodge Critical Rare Earths Project in the Black Hills National Forest in northeastern Wyoming, with a goal of project commissioning in late 2016. Our focused exploration work over the past eight years has given America a growing, longlife rare earth district, with competitive grades of heavy and critical rare earths. With timely permitting and advancement of the Forest Service's ongoing Environmental Impact Statement (EIS), we believe the Bear Lodge Project can be America's primary source of critical rare earths beginning in 2016, making it a significant, valuable and secure domestic complement to the production from Molycorp's Mountain Pass Mine that is more weighted in the lighter rare earth elements.

Mine commissioning at the Bear Lodge Project by 2016, while possible, is not assured. The EIS process has begun, and the Bear Lodge Project deserves a high level of urgency on the part of the Forest Service to complete the NEPA process in an accelerated and streamlined fashion.

The Department of Energy has expressed the need to "accelerate and streamline" the federal permitting process through the entire critical minerals supply chain, beginning with mining. In his Global Threat Assessment to the Senate Intelligence Committee in March 2013, the Director of National Intelligence specifically cited "regulatory hurdles" as a factor limiting the United States' ability to counter China's monopoly on rare earth elements.

We call for no shortcuts. Rather, focused attention, accelerated and streamlined urgency will allow the Forest Service to provide a Record of Decision by early 2016, leading to construction, commissioning and first production. This Committee is urged to stress to the Forest Service the importance of meeting this 2016 goal.

Why the Bear Lodge Project has become a Critical National Resource

- The Bull Hill Mine near Sundance, WY and the hydrometallurgy plant at nearby Upton, WY combine to be North America's most advanced rare earths development project.
- The mine has a small footprint of less than 900 acres in an excellent location with adjacent infrastructure, power, transportation, skilled labor and strong local and statewide support.
- It is poised to begin production of 5,000 -10,000 tons of rare earths annually by late 2016.

- The Bear Lodge Project will be a viable, secure domestic source of such critical rare earths as Neodymium, Dysprosium, Europium, Yttrium and Terbium for at least 25 years.
- The Forest Service has chosen the EIS Project Manager and third-party EIS contractor, and expects to produce a Draft EIS in 4Q 2014 and a final Record of Decision in 1Q 2016.
- Growth potential in the Bear Lodge Rare Earths district is excellent, with adjacent exploration targets indicating further heavy rare earth enrichment.
- Multiple economic and strategic benefits can come from the Company's patent-pending metallurgical processing technology that produces a 97 percent pure-bulk rare-earths concentrate that is free of uranium and thorium.
- The process technology also enables process chemical recycling and regeneration, giving lower capital and operating expenses as well as a zero-discharge hydrometallurgy facility and small tailings footprint.
- Evaluation of rare earth elemental separation from the concentrate has begun.
- Rare Element Resources has entered into a non-disclosure agreement with the DOE's Ames and Idaho National Laboratories under the auspices of DOE's Critical Materials Institute for rare earths separation research.
- The detailed design and economic analysis portions of the Feasibility Study have begun.

Innovative American mining companies such as Rare Element Resources need a timely "Yes" or "No" after we have invested private capital, talent and innovation to identify domestic resources and technologies that can help answer America's critical minerals needs. S. 1600 is a bold step toward ensuring that federal agencies can have the financial and personnel resources they need, and for these reasons Rare Element Resources strongly supports S.1600 and urges its prompt passage.

Rare Element Resources Ltd. is a publicly traded mineral resource company focused on exploration and development of rare earth deposits, specifically those with significant distribution of critical rare earths. Headquartered in Lakewood, CO, the company was incorporated in 1999. Its common shares are traded on the New York Stock Exchange Market (the "NYSE MKT") under the symbo "EE" and on the Toronto Stock Exchange (the "TSX") under the symbol "RES."

STATEMENT OF KEN COLLISON, CHIEF OPERATING OFFICER, UCORE RARE METALS,

This is written testimony submitted for the hearing record on S.1600, the Critical Minerals Policy Act. My name is Ken Collison, Chief Operating Officer for Ucore Rare Metals, Inc. (Ucore). Ucore is actively developing the Bokan- Dotson Ridge Rare Earth Project (project) located on Prince of Wales Island in Southeast Alaska. The project is in the final stages of evaluation and design and is anticipating initiating the NEPA permitting review process early in 2014. The Bokan- Dotson Ridge project is particularly enriched with heavy rare earth elements, including the critical elements Dysprosium, Terbium and Yttrium. Approximately 40 percent (by weight) of the rare earth elements contained on the Dotson Ridge property are heavy rare earths elements, as disclosed in the Company's Nl43-101 compliant Preliminary Economic Assessment, released in January 2013.

Ucore sincerely appreciates the recent initiatives in Washington to address the increasing lack of availability of rare earth products and magnet-making materials for domestic military and defense applications. Concerns regarding the withdrawal of ongoing supplies of Critical Rare Earth Oxides produced almost exclusively in China and consumed by US military contractors, has attracted significant legislative initiatives.

The Critical Minerals Policy Act, submitted by Senators Lisa Murkowski (R- AK), Ron Wyden (D- Ore), Mark Udall (D- Col.), Dean Heller (R- Nev.) and 13 others, if fully enacted, will prevent supply shortages of critical materials and reduce US dependence on foreign sources through the revitalization of a domestic supply chain, including domestic production from near term facilities such as the BokanDotson Ridge project in Alaska. The bipartisan bill outlines mineral-specific actions for several elements, including yttrium and scandium, materials scheduled to commence production at the Bokan project by as early as 2017.

Dotson Ridge is the richest domestic source of three heavy rare earth elements-dysprosium, terbium, and yttrium-which are critical to several advanced weapon systems, such as stealth helicopters and precision-guided weapons. Both dysprosium and yttrium are critical to multiple US defense systems. Dysprosium is a crucial ingredient in neodymium-iron-boron magnets as a means of increasing coercivity, applications of which include aircraft actuator motors in flight control systems, landing gear, and munitions. Yttrium is critical to the defense industry applications such as the manufacture of various ceramic and glass materials required in jet engines. The Joint Strike Fighter (JSF) development program relies on both Dy andY as critical input components.

Currently, all of the world's commercially-available heavy rare earth elements are produced in China. Ongoing production and export quotas have limited the availability of these materials to global markets. According to a March 2012 report from DOD, yttrium, terbium, and dysprosium are all considered to be "critical to the production, sustainment, or operation of significant United States military equipment," as well as "subject to interruption of supply, based on actions or events outside the control of the government of the United States." Yttrium, in particular, was shown to be in deficit when considering projected future domestic supply.

Thank you for the opportunity to submit testimony on this important bill.

STATEMENT OF DENNIS WATSON, MAYOR, CITY OF CRAIG, ALASKA

This is written testimony submitted for the hearing record on S.1600, the Critical Minerals Policy Act. My name is Dennis Watson, Mayor of Craig, Alaska located on Prince of Wales Island in Southeast Alaska. Craig has a population of 1200 and is the largest community on America's third largest island which has a total population of 4,000. There are total of ten communities on the island, many of which are connected by road to one another as a result of the road system built during the better days of timber harvest.

I mention these roads because my testimony on this bill is about the need to evaluate surface transportation access to American sites that can supply critical minerals including rare earth minerals. As the Committee knows, Alaska is blessed with an abundance of minerals which it has supplied to the Nation since it was acquired from Russia in the 19th century. Southeast Alaska and Prince of Wales have historically been part of this tradition, and a number of successful mines have been developed on the Island.

Now, there is a great prospect for development of new mines on Prince of Wales Island. One of these is a potential rare earth mineral mine which could provide a lot of rare earth minerals to our nation's economy and security. That mine is called the Bokan-Dotson Ridge project.

> "The Bokan property is particularly enriched with heavy rare earth elements, including the critical elements Dysprosium, Terbium and Yttrium. Approximately 40 percent(by weight) of the rare earth elements contained on the Dotson Ridge property are heavy rare earths elements, as disclosed in the Company's NI43-101 compliant resource estimate, released in March of 2011." See http://ucore.com/projects/bokan-mountain-alaska/project-overviewSo and attachment

So, the development of this property has great potential for the nation and is just what Sen. Murkowski and the cosponsors of this bill intend that the study authorized by this bill evaluate. The City of Craig strongly supports the Bokan—Dotson Ridge project and has requested the Alaska Congressional delegation to sponsor a bill, S.181, to allow surface transportation access to the mine site. As I said above, Prince of Wales has an extensive road system, more than most places in rural Alaska. However, even though the Bokan-Dotson Ridge project is located on Prince of Wales Island, there is no road connecting the project site with the rest of the POW road system. Even more frustrating is the fact that the current state of federal land management most likely prevents construction of a road without specific legislation action by this Committee because much of the area on which a road could be sited is now located in a Roadless area since over 90 percent of Southeast Alaska has been declared" roadless" by an ill-advised federal court decision which voided a long standing out of court settlement that had exempted Southeast Alaska from the rest of the nation's roadless issues.

We urge this committee to do two things:

1. Please include a study of transportation issues for critical minerals , particularly rare-earth minerals in this bill. This bill is intended to identify how the United States may find and develop a secure, domestic supply of these critical minerals. However, if the minerals exist but federal land management policy prevents or substantially retards the ability to develop and transport these mineral to a logical production site, then this policy needs to be identified in this report and needs to be adjusted to accommodate these needs.

The Study should identify these access problems and recommend specific changes to allow these critical/rare earth minerals to be developed with logical and economic access.

2. Please schedule a hearing on S.181 which provides a solution for this specific surface transportation problem for the critical rare earth minerals at Bokan-Dotson Ridge. That bill is a bipartisan bill which was introduced by Ranking Member Murkowski and Sen. Begich almost a year ago, January 30, 2013, Yet, there has been no hearing on this bill. There has been a hearing on the companion bill, HR. 587 in the House Natural Resources Committee and we are hoping that the bill will be marked up soon.

The bills are identical and are very simple-they provide an exception to the Roadless Rule To permit construction of a road between the Bokan- Dotson Ridge project and another precious metals mine. The bill does not authorize and funding for construction. The bill seeks only to solve the Roadless problem. It is not an earmark for road construction. The mine's sponsors understand and support this bill. They are not looking for federal subsidy but the mine needs this surface access to make its transportation more viable and to allow Prince of Wales Island residents to work as employees.

Additionally, this would allow local residents of the island to obtain year round employment at the mine. Right now the only access is by boat which is just not very practical for daily commuting from communities on the Island which has an annual unemployment rate of 12.8 percent through November 2013..

Attached for the record are many letters and resolutions of support from all over the State and region. This project is supported by local communities which form the Prince of Wales Community Advisory Council and encompass most of the communities on the Island as well as the Southeast Conference and Ketchikan and Alaska State Chambers of Commerce. In summary, the Bokan-Dotson Ridge mineral prospect has a real chance to make a difference in America's rare earth mineral supply. But the Committee and the Congress need to look directly at the surface transportation issues affecting this and other mineral properties.

Thank you for the opportunity to submit testimony on this important bill. I hope that I will have the opportunity soon to testify at a similar hearing on S.181, and hopefully in person.

○

www.ingramcontent.com/pod-product-compliance
Lightning Source LLC
Chambersburg PA
CBHW081843280526
45789CB00007B/2553

* 9 7 8 1 5 0 0 7 3 7 5 4 2 *